*How to Use Houseplants Indoors
for Beauty and Decoration*

How to Use Houseplants Indoors for Beauty and Decoration

JACK KRAMER and
ANDREW R. ADDKISON, A.I.D.

DOUBLEDAY & COMPANY, INC.
GARDEN CITY, NEW YORK
1974

All photos by Max Eckert unless otherwise credited.

Book design by M. F. Gazze

Frontis: Room design by Larry Mulscher.

Library of Congress Cataloging in Publication Data

Kramer, Jack, 1927–
    How to use houseplants indoors for beauty and decoration.

    1. House plants in interior decoration.
I. Addkison, Andrew, joint author.   II. Title.
SB419.K713   747'.9
ISBN 0-385-01415-5
Library of Congress Catalog Card Number 74–1771

Contents

Introduction: Living with Plants

In the last ten years indoor plants have become as much a part of homes and apartments as drapery or furniture. Many plants once restricted to conservatory growing now thrive indoors because sophisticated heating and humidity systems have become available to most home owners. Today, indoor plants are as important to a room as their counterparts outdoors are to the yard. Specimen plants (large mature species) for indoor decoration are now available from many sources and are used both for beauty and as structural design elements in a room. Philodendrons and dieffenbachias and lacy seven-foot trees such as *Ficus benjamina* are all part of the plant-in-home usage. So are large flowering plants such as hibiscus and orchids. Large cacti and succulents are other notable examples

This contemporary room relies on the bold effect of the specimen palm to make it complete, and the fern atop the bookcase makes a fitting crown of green to a very well designed room. (Wayne James, Designer)

of today's indoor plants. Some plants are expensive—palms, for example—others are moderate in price. In any case, selection, placement, and care of plants are vital parts of a complete decorating or design service.

While there are many books on houseplants, few of them treat the plant as a design element in the home and what it can do for a room in relation to shape, mass, and color. In this book we not only tell you how to use plants effectively indoors, but also how to select them, where to find them, and how to care for them for maximum beauty.

We have selected over a hundred of the best indoor plants—new ones and old favorites—and no matter if you have an apartment or a house, in this book you will find plants to decorate your rooms and to brighten every day of your life.

Jack Kramer
Andrew R. Addkison, A.I.D.

*How to Use Houseplants Indoors
for Beauty and Decoration*

1 🍃

Using Houseplants Effectively

Today's indoor plants include many new, extravagantly beautiful species that add interest to any room of the home. Whether in living room or kitchen, bath or hall, a living plant can be—if chosen carefully —as much a part of the total room as a chair or table. A tall *Ficus benjamina* (banyan tree) adds grace and beauty to any area. Hanging baskets of plectranthus (Swedish ivy), their handsome scalloped leaves a halo of green, can substitute for drapery against a window wall. And dramatic bromeliads in vibrant colors can act as lacquered vases on a table or desk.

This beautiful contemporary living room relies on organic materials to make it attractive, and plants are right at home. The philodendron on the balcony is balanced by another philodendron at the fireplace. Dried leaves in vases against the fireplace add another type of plant material and a pair of gesneriads decorating the tables continues the flow of greenery. (Hedrich Blessing photo; Alden B. Dow & Assoc., Architects)

*In a dining area, pots of begonias in matching containers
provide color and beauty at a window. (Matthew Barr photo)*

2 ❧ *How to Use Houseplants Indoors for Beauty and Decoration*

The new indoor array of living plants—even such old favorites as philodendrons and dieffenbachias—are more than plants: They are design elements as well as color accents in a room. Gone is the plant once used "as a touch of green"; now we use plants in a much different way. They are selected and arranged in the same manner as outdoor plants, that is, to fulfill a need and to establish a mood or refine a setting.

Just any plant will no longer do in today's home or apartment. You want a plant that can, by its color or leaf texture, growth habit or attitude, provide or do something for a room much in the same manner a piece of furniture does. And indeed, some of the large plants (called specimen-sized plants) cost as much as furniture. Interior designers and plantsmen realize the importance of living plants for interiors. And suppliers have rallied to the demand with unique plants of uncommon beauty for homes. So why not use them?

SOME FAVORITE HOUSEPLANTS

Favorite houseplants of the past have been philodendrons, ivy, and dieffenbachias, and you might think they were chosen for special characteristics: resistance to insects, beauty of leaf or flower, or perhaps ease of culture. Unfortunately, this was not the case; these plants became popular because they were easily propagated and available. Yet most philodendrons become straggly with time, ivy almost invariably attracts spider mites (even under ideal conditions), and dieffenbachias wilt in the slightest draft. There are some fine varieties of philodendron and dieffenbachia that can tolerate untoward conditions (none of ivy, I am sorry to say), but generally these old favorites are not stellar candidates for indoor living. They are overrated when you consider the dozens of other fine indoor plants that have so much to offer, for example, ferns and palms, cacti and succulents, and so forth.

Bromeliads with their unusual foliage and brightly colored flowers make fine houseplants, good for table accents. This group includes aechmeas, guzmanias, and neoregelias. (Photo courtesy Fennell Orchids) ABOVE

A pair of magnificent fiddleleaf figs (Ficus lyrata) flank an entryway. Palms and seasonal "mums" carry the line to create an impressive picture. (Larry Mulscher, Designer) RIGHT

For years the retail customer has been warned by florists and nursery-men to avoid flowering plants such as camellias and orchids in the home. Yet with proper care these plants live and thrive for years indoors. What is more pleasant on a gray November day than red hibiscus flowers, or a bouquet of yellow orchids? So if flowering plants are your favorites, by all means have them!

Bromeliads are other dandy indoor plants that add much to any room. They are almost care-free and will not die if you forget to water them for a few weeks. And even in shaded corners there are bromeliads to add beauty to the home.

If you prefer lush green foliage plants—and some rooms demand them rather than flowering ones—select carefully because there are many. *Ficus benjamina* (banyan tree) is lacy and delicate; *Ficus lyrata* (the fiddle-leaf fig) is bold and massive. *Schefflera (Brassaia) actinophylla* (umbrella tree) is a lovely green canopy, but remember that this is a tall plant which does not achieve its beauty until mature, and if you do not have an eight-foot ceiling, forget it!

If philodendrons are part of your past and you want to use them, choose one of the self-heading types such as *Philodendron wendlandii*, which is an immense rosette of apple-green leaves. In the right place in the right room it is stunning. Avoid the vine-type philodendrons such as *P. cordatum* that never amount to much and bring more grief than glory to an area. If the room needs a touch of drama, use *P. pertusum* (the Swiss cheese plant), with its large scalloped leaves. In the evening, properly lighted, its silhouette against a wall makes it something special.

DESIGN AND PLANTS

Plants should play a part in the design (or decoration) of various rooms right from the start. Too often the owner asks, "Where shall I put a few plants?" *after* a room has been completed. By then there is seldom a place for one plant, much less two. The spaces we live in have the personality we give them; that is, we choose the furniture, wall hangings, plants, et cetera. For example, a floral crewel sofa cover or an antique oriental rug play a certain role in creating a specific character; the same is true when choosing plants and their containers.

Plants can serve as mass to anchor a grouping of furniture or provide airy, visual patterns above a window seat—and myriad roles in between. Trial and error in buying plants is often costly and frustrating, causing people to mutter that they have a brown thumb. It is far better to plan for plants and to choose correct, healthy ones at the outset for the conditions and specific needs of the room.

LINE

It is necessary to understand a few design terms to know where to put your plant and what kind of plant to use. One important aspect of room design is line. To understand line, squint your eyes and look at a fern—you will find it forms a fountain shape. Now imagine a yardstick placed on top of the plant. If that yardstick is exactly the same height as the back of a sofa, the fern would extend the line of the sofa if placed next to the sofa; this is a functional use of a plant. Plants used in this way add dimension to a room because they are part of the design.

MASS

Again squint your eyes. The sofa, plants, and, if there is one, lamp become a mass that is an aggregation of objects which assumes a shape. This creates a somewhat low, horizontal mass. Rooms are composed of a combination of masses or shapes. Two chairs with a table between them would also form a mass of a different shape.

*A corner with dieffenbachias—bold and massive—helps create
balance with the large sofa in this living room and brings into
the room the outdoors beyond the windows.* ABOVE

*Plants in this entrance immediately give the visitor a welcome.
The tall bamboo is stellar in its place. Ferns and other green plants
add horizontal thrust. (Delano Constantine, Designer)* LEFT

FORM

Another word for shape, form is defined in geometric terms. For example, we say a Christmas tree is pyramidal or cone-shaped, its leaves are oval, round, or elliptical, and so forth. Often it is pleasing to play one form against another similar form, such as tall arching palms in front of tall arching windows. Or you can use dissimilar forms that oppose each other, such as a very horizontal straight-backed sofa with a vertical palm.

TEXTURE AND SCALE

These are probably the most important aspects of good design; each relates to the other. Scale is the relationship of one thing to another, whether it be texture, size, or form. Scale is used in many, often illusionary, ways to our advantage. Suppose you are standing between two rows of pole beans in your garden: The leaves close to you are large and defined, but those at the other end of the row are small and become only a texture to the eye. Thus a fine-textured plant like a small-leaved ficus placed at one end of a room and a large-leaved ficus placed near the entrance of the room fool a person's eye when he enters by creating an illusion that the small-leaved plant is farther away than it really is. Thus this tends to make the room seem larger. If you reverse the plants, the opposite occurs: The room looks smaller.

As mentioned, scale also relates to size and form; a peacock is beautiful, but can you imagine one in a canary-bird cage? The scale would be inappropriate. Often you see an overgrown rubber tree or fiddleleaf fig in a room with a standard eight-foot ceiling. The plant has grown up against the ceiling and starts bending over, searching for light. It is out of

Bamboo is the important plant here, lacy and frilly and softening to the sharp, geometric architectural lines. (M. Morrison, Designer)

Cacti can appear like sculpture in a room; this fine specimen is Trichocereus species and brings color and drama to a corner. (Photo by Matthew Barr)

12 ❧ *How to Use Houseplants Indoors for Beauty and Decoration*

This apartment dining room niche relies on a pair of palms to unify two areas, and the placement of the plants—one in rear and one in the front—makes the area seem larger. Their height and airiness contrasts nicely with the low, massive table and seating arrangement. (Dean Reynolds, Designer)

Using Houseplants Effectively ❦ *13*

scale with the room. Another example is an African violet on a grand piano. The beauty of the small violet is lost against the largeness of the piano.

When you combine line, mass, form, color, and scale, you have the elements that dictate the character of the room. Each one relates to the other to provide a total harmonious space.

COLOR

Color is complex and we can only skim the surface so you will understand why we select a certain plant for its color rather than a different plant. When we select a plant we must relate the color of that plant to the color of the room. Color involves light and how it reflects or strikes surfaces (in the daytime a room assumes different colors), value which is the light or dark of color, and coolness (meaning blues and greens) and warmness (meaning reds and yellows) and values thereof.

Basically plants will be in rooms in two different light conditions: daylight and artificial. To determine the color range of a room study the color value relationships of the space. Some rooms appear light and warm, other rooms appear cool and dark.

Most houseplants are green but green varies in its tones from the dark green leaves of the rubber plant to the chartreuse green fronds of the maidenhair fern. The rubber plant leaf is leathery and dark green, almost opaque, and since no light passes through the leaf it appears dark. The fern frond on the other hand allows light to pass through it, making it somewhat translucent or a lighter green.

If you have a combination of furnishings of dark rich color, use dark-valued plants—dark greens, purple-greens, blue-greens—to carry further the dark values of the room to create harmony. If the room is all dark-valued, light green plants (yellow-green, apple-green) would create an equally dramatic effect because of contrasts. If the room is light or of

*A living room corner relies on plants to complete the
southwestern ambiance of this total scene. Lacy ferns and palms
are used in combination with a sleek cleistocactus behind the
natural browns and rusts of the sofa; and alongside the brick
and stone fireplace is another cactus,* Cereus peruvianus,
*providing both green color and rugged form against the stark
white of the fireplace. (Photo by Matthew Barr; Andrew R.
Addkison, Designer)*

A single, large philodendron is used as an accent in this living room area. It serves two purposes: to create a natural division between the two areas and to provide dark green color for a pastel wall. (Harold Grieve, Designer)

middle values of neutral colors, a dark green plant is usually overbearing and causes too much drama. In other words, the eye sees the plant before what is in the room. In these cases it is better to use a middle-to-light-valued plant to blend with the rest of the room. (In any case, lighting would be a determining factor.)

PLACING PLANTS

The interiors of most apartments and homes are rectangular-shaped areas filled with furnishings. The sofa is usually necessary not only for seating but as a large mass to act as a starting point for placement of other furniture in the room. Often the sofa is on the long wall because that is the only place in the room that can handle it. It will then be either perpendicular to the fireplace (if there is one) or on the opposite wall, parallel to it. If perpendicularly placed, the couch should be far enough away from the wall to leave room for an end table and lamp with leftover space at the corner. The temptation in this situation is to fill the space with a plant. One plant here would not do the job because it would be awkward and look like it was just stuck there to fill space. This is the corner for a large plant *and a few smaller ones* to form a cone or pyramidal mass that moves the eye down to the lamp and then the sofa and on the other side down to the mantel or fireplace itself. Remember that there must be windows nearby to provide light. In your group of plants strive for contrasts in texture and value to create interest: for example, a large fiddleleaf fig in the corner with a pair of *Dracaena warnecki* at two heights. Fill in with low ferns to carry the line of the sofa back. This way you are integrating the plants with the furnishings rather than just placing plants in a room. (A room with one plant grouping in it is like a room with only a single wall picture.) Now balance with other plants in the room.

Generally ferns are out of place in a very formal room because they are natural flowing plants, hardly trimmed or manicured. Symmetrical, well-trained plants with large leaves and smooth texture are more appropriate. They can be centered in front of window walls (each plant the same height, mass, and shape). They become an element of design when used in a repetitious manner. However, be sure the tops of the plants are in line with the other objects in the room, such as lamp shades and bookcases, to provide relationship between objects.

If the living room is very large and not rectangularly shaped, study the space carefully and imagine planting groups that may be seen from all sides (freestanding). If the room already has horizontal emphasis, such as beams or cornices, think in terms of a row of plants. If the room has angular emphasis, such as slanted or hipped ceilings, use a plant group, or repeat these lines. If the ceiling is vaulted or cathedral-shaped, use cascading plants like arching palms to create harmony. In other words, play one similar form against another to create interest.

Plants are used intelligently in this handsome room; the tall tree-type cordyline at right moves the eye to the smaller palm creating perspective. The addition of the flower arrangement above the seating group completes the harmonious setting. (John Hall, Designer)

2

How to Select Plants

Room or decorator plants come in many sizes, shapes, and kinds. Some are slender and graceful, while others are bold and massive. Some have tiny leaves, others have broad leaves. Some are pyramidal in shape; others are branching. It is not enough to select a plant just because it looks pretty; it must fit the place you have for it; so when picking plants for interiors, consider the following factors:

Size of plant
Shape and growth habit of plant
Size and color of leaves
Character of plant

Palms are graceful and elegant and here are used as a vertical accent to frame a window. Their fountain shape is especially desirable in rooms. (Reginald Adams, Designer)

Rubber trees (Ficus elastica decora) *are favorite plants and make fine vertical accents for rooms, especially for areas receiving little light. Some species can grow to ten feet.* (Photo by Matthew Barr)

PLANT SIZE

Like clothing, plants come in many different sizes: small, medium, large, and extra large. The size you select depends upon how much space you have for the specific plant. In other words, each space will dictate the size of the plant.

For simplicity we can classify plants as small: to 18 inches; medium: to 36 inches; large: to 48 inches; and very large, tree-type plants: 48 inches to 100 inches. (The very large plants are sometimes referred to as specimen or select plants, which means they are mature and at the peak of form.) We can carry the classifications one step further: Small plants will be in 5- to 7-inch pots, medium ones in 8- to 12-inch containers, large ones in 12- to 20-inch tubs, and very large or tree-type plants in tubs over 20 inches.

You can, of course, buy a medium-sized plant and grow it into a large one, but most people buy the size of plant they need at the moment for a specific area. (However, if plant prices keep soaring, this pattern may change.) A specimen plant, say a treelike ficus or a columnar eight-foot cactus, may cost as much as $150, and palms at $150 are not uncommon. However, many fine medium-sized plants are offered at reasonable prices, from $15 to $25.

If cost is a factor, use a medium plant on a pedestal in place of a specimen plant. Tables and plant pedestals are sold at salvage stores; you may find some lovely old ones that were once used for ferns. There are now new pedestal stands on the market, too.

SHAPE AND HABIT OF PLANT

The plant you see in a dealer's shop may not yet be mature, so it will be difficult to know its ultimate height or appearance because many plants change drastically in character between the young and mature stages. For

example, some plants, like *Dracaena marginata*, when young, hardly resemble the lovely mature plant that has large thrusting branches crowned with a cluster of spear-shaped leaves; the youngster is merely one or two branches not yet assuming its graceful shape.

Palms too can be deceptive when young and do not look like the plant they become at maturity. *Howea forsteriana* (the kentia palm), a favorite decorator plant, ultimately grows into a lovely fountain shape, but *Rhapis excelsa* (the lady palm) stays low and massive, more clustering than vertical. *Chamaedorea erumpens* (the bamboo palm) sends out side shoots, becoming massy and frilly as time goes on, thus losing its vertical stalky appearance.

For simplicity we can say that a plant is branching, treelike, fountain, canopy, or rosette shaped. Or it can be a cascading or trailing plant. Try to select a plant that is in contrast to the lines of a room and its furnishings. For example, if a room is very square and angular, a fountain-shaped plant or canopy type will add softness to the room. Or exaggerate the linear space of such a room with tall vertical treelike plants. (Space for the plant, as mentioned, will be a determining factor.)

Following is a listing of a few plants in these various categories (complete plant lists in Chapter 5):

BRANCHING
    Araucaria excelsa (Norfolk pine)
    Clusia rosea
    Euphorbia lactea (candelabra plant)
    Ficus lyrata (fiddleleaf fig)
    Philodendron pertusum (Swiss cheese plant)
    P. selloum (fingerleaf philodendron)
    Trichocereus (many species)

A fishtail palm (Caryota mitis) *provides sparse elegance for a corner. Because of their varied shapes and generally undemanding requirements, several species of the palm are fine for room decoration. (Photo by Matthew Barr)*

TREELIKE
> *Cordyline terminalis* (ti plant)
> *Dracaena massangeana* (decorator plant)
> *Ficus elastica decora* (rubber tree)

FOUNTAIN SHAPE
> *Beaucarnea recurvata* (ponytail plant)
> *Cycas revoluta* (sago palm)
> *Dieffenbachia amoena* (dumbcane)
> *Howea forsteriana* (kentia palm)

CANOPY
> *Schefflera (Brassaia) actinophylla* (umbrella tree)
> *Dizygotheca elegantissima* (spider aralia)
> *Fatsia japonica*
> *Polyscias fruticosa* (ming tree)

ROSETTE
> Agave (many kinds)
> *Asplenium nidus* (bird's-nest fern)
> *Dracaena warnecki*
> *Guzmania lingulata*
> *Neoregelia carolinae*

CASCADING
> *Aeschynanthus speciosus* (lipstick vine)
> *Asparagus sprengeri* (emerald fern)
> *Begonia limminghiana*
> *Cissus rhombifolia* (grape ivy)
> *Dendrobium pierardii*
> *Saxifraga sarmentosa* (strawberry geranium)

LEAF SIZE AND COLOR

There is incredible variation in leaf shape and size. Some plants have tiny leaves, others have large ones. Some plants have fronds while others have spear-shaped foliage. The shape and size of the leaf together with the shape of the plant give it its character. A large-leaved plant is invariably bold in appearance and makes a definite statement, whereas a lacy-leaved plant is graceful and delicate in character. For example, in a small room the large-leaved *Ficus elastica* (rubber tree) would be out of scale with the rest of the room, but a small-leaved plant like *Ficus benjamina* (banyan tree) is ideal.

Plants with scalloped leaves (for example, many philodendrons) look more decorative than plants with straight-edged leaves because the curves and cutouts appeal to the eye. Small-leaved plants like polyscias look frilly and might be fine in one room but out of character in another area. Palms tend to be lush and dark green and give an area a tropical note, which is often desirable. (Ironically, palms blend with contemporary as well as traditional settings.)

Color, too, makes a difference in the character of a plant. Green is not simply green; there are many shades and tones. Some plants are dark green, and others, like *Dracaena massangeana*, are almost apple-green. Dark-leaved plants appear heavy and massive, but lighter green plants appear more graceful and airy.

Because of their growth habit and leaf form, some plants appear majestic, almost regal. *Cordyline terminalis* in tree form is an example, as are yuccas and *Dracaena marginata*. They add a note of elegance in a room. *Dizygotheca elegantissima* (spider aralia) has an oriental flavor; its leaves are like delicate Japanese brush strokes against a white wall. Some plants look almost like sculpture in a room; large agaves and trichocereus cacti are prime examples. *Philodendron pertusum* (Swiss cheese plant) is definitely tropical in appearance, and other plants, like *Chamaerops humilis* (the fan palm) are spiky looking.

Small-leaved plants can add a lovely tapestry texture to a room. This shows a closeup of the beautiful fronds of a fern. (Photo by Jack Barnish) LEFT

The rosette or fountain shape of a dieffenbachia is shown in this photo. These are large-leaved bold character plants and generally need plenty of space to be at their best, although since they are not demanding about light, they can be used in areas where other plants might not survive. (Photo by Matthew Barr) RIGHT

Large agaves make beautiful houseplants for table or floor and
bring the less common star or rosette shape into the home.
These plants come in many different colors so choose
accordingly. (Photo by Joyce R. Wilson)

WHERE TO BUY PLANTS

Years ago, if you wanted an indoor plant your choice was limited as to the types of plants and where you could buy them, but today there are hundreds of good room plants and many places to get them. Some stores are specifically devoted to houseplants, and the garden sections of department stores, most nurseries and patio shops, and mail-order companies that ship large tropical plants all offer houseplants. Let us look at these sources and see what they specifically offer.

FLORIST SHOPS

Most large florists in big cities have a fair selection of the more standard larger treelike plants: philodendrons, ficus, cacti, and occasionally orchids. Plants will be of high quality and high price. Most florists will generally replace a large plant if anything goes wrong with it after you have had it a few months and have given it reasonable care. But do not expect a florist to replace the plant if you have mishandled or mistreated it or have had it over a year.

PATIO SHOPS AND NURSERIES

These large establishments have houseplants, but generally the bulk of their business is outdoor nursery stock such as trees and shrubs, annuals and perennials. Thus selection may not be great, but prices will be moderate to high. You will usually find more table and desk plants like begonias and cissus and a few palms and ferns here. Also, most of these stores have a good selection of hanging plants.

I have generally found that nurseries and patio attendants do not know too much about houseplants, and if you run into trouble after the plant is home, you are more or less on your own. Remember that their

The Australian umbrella tree (Schefflera [Brassaia] acontifolia)
*has a canopy shape, well suited to its place here, where it brings
curving lines to soften the straight lines of the stone fireplace.*
(*Photo by Molly Adams*)

32 ❧ *How to Use Houseplants Indoors for Beauty and Decoration*

business is usually nursery stock. Still, all in all, the patio or nursery is not a bad place to buy your indoor plants if you know what you want and how to grow it.

HOUSEPLANT STORES

In these specialty stores the owners generally know their plants well, sell high quality, and depend upon your word-of-mouth business to keep them in business. Thus, they do everything possible to give you the best plants. Here you will find an exceptional selection, from cacti to foliage to flowering beauties. Prices are apt to be high, but, as mentioned, you get service and advice if plants go wrong later.

In most large cities these houseplant specialty stores have sprung up with great zest. Recently in Chicago (after not visiting for a year) I found seven of these stores in one shopping day. In New York, too, many have opened, as well as in St. Louis, and in San Francisco there are an incredible number. So perhaps these are the places to get your larger plants. Some of these shops also offer maintenance service for plants (they will come to your home a few times a month to maintain plants for a fee), and others will even rent the plant by the month rather than selling outright.

MAIL-ORDER SUPPLIERS

I want to stress that if you cannot get to a large city and want a big plant, do not be defeated; buy from one of the mail-order places. These suppliers offer a good selection of plants. They know how to ship plants (even the biggest), overnight air mail shipment is good, and in most cases the packing of plants is done well. Thus you are quite safe ordering from these suppliers. Once again, however, the watchword here is that you must know your plant, that is, its botanical name, to get what you

The fiddleleaf fig (Ficus lyrata) *is vertical as well as branching in habit and makes an excellent plant where size and shape are of importance.* (*Photo courtesy Architectural Pottery Co.*)

want. If possible, send for catalogs first because they will help you identify plants.

Here is a list of some of the suppliers I have dealt with through the years. It is not a large list and does not mean that other suppliers are not as good. These are merely the companies I know and have done business with and from whom I have always received good plants.

HOUSEPLANT SUPPLIERS

Alberts & Merkel Bros., Inc.
P. O. Box 537
Boynton Beach, FL 33435

Burgess Seed & Plant Co., Inc.
67 E. Battle Creek St.
Galesburg, MI 49053

Kartuz Greenhouses
92 Chestnut St.
Wilmington, MA 01887

Logee's Greenhouses
55 North St.
Danielson, CT 06239

Merry Gardens
Camden, ME 04843

George W. Park Seed Co., Inc.
Box 31
Greenwood, SC 29646

Tinari Greenhouses
2325 Valley Rd.
Bethayres, PA 19006

HOW TO TELL A GOOD PLANT
FROM A BAD ONE

Quality is a big word these days, not only in general merchandise but also in plants. Some plants are perfectly grown over a long period in ideal conditions. Other plants are force-fed to grow the most in the quickest time; the result is that when you get the plant home it generally succumbs in a short time. Although it is difficult to tell the good from the bad in plants, there are a few indicators. Avoid a plant that has wan or limp leaves; leaves should be perky and bright green. The stem should be solid and rigid, not limp. The plant should have a fresh look, just like good fruit, rather than a bruised or off-color appearance.

Also check plants for insects. Look on underside of leaves and in leaf axils for these pests. If you see them, do *not* buy the plant under any circumstance. Another helpful hint is to check the soil. Yes, feel the soil; if it is dry and caky, the plant has been around a long time, so avoid it. If there are brown or white streaks on leaves, avoid the plant because it might have rot or another disease. If leaf edges are chewed, you know some insect has been at work and might still be harbored in the soil.

Remember that there is no Better Business Bureau for houseplants, and once you buy them, they are yours, so take your time. Look, observe, and inspect plants before you purchase so you will have healthy plants with which to decorate your rooms.

3 🍂

Plants as Decorative Elements

Today plants are structural design elements of a room. Like a wall hanging or a piece of sculpture, they provide vertical accent or a horizontal thrust to carry the eye from one area to another. A plant may flank a fireplace, bring beauty to a bare corner, or act as a dramatic silhouette against a wall. A plant can also be used to guide traffic in a room and to complement furnishings. One or two plants may also serve as an accessory for a table or desk to provide a spot of beauty to harmonize with other, larger plants in the room. Window gardens are still with us, and in the right areas—kitchen, dining room—they are fine. Plants set on pedestals are also good decoration for almost any room.

Plants growing up through the floor! In this case an excellent idea.
The palm is actually in a plant well and appears like a tree,
covering a large wall with greenery. (Hunter-White Interiors)

So no matter what the room or the location—at windows, on tables or pedestals, or used as structural elements (floor plants)—there are plants for all places; it is simply a matter of choosing the right one for the right spot.

TABLE AND DESK PLANTS

A plant in a 4- to 6-inch pot is an ideal decoration for table or desk because it is the finishing touch. Seek unique, colorful, well-kept specimens, not too large to smother the table or too small to be inconspicuous. Use plants on tables and desks as you would a vase or a bowl. Their beauty should be understated, but important and pleasing in all aspects. Select plants that pick up the other colors in the room to create a total scene. If the walls are dark, use brightly colored flowering plants to act

An ordinary table plant can be used as an unusual vase. Here a dark green-leaved bromeliad holds brilliantly contrasting fresh red carnations. ABOVE

A pair of beautifully flowering African violets accent an end table and carry the line of the sofa. The rosette shape of the plants blends well with the graceful curves of the lamp, and both the foliage and flowers add color. (Joyce R. Wilson photo)

as contrasts. Ornamental containers for desk plants are a must. Do not pot directly in them; use the pot-in-a-pot method: into a handsome cache pot, brass container, or whatever suits the room best.

Provide furniture with adequate protection against water stain. Look for special saucers with cork liners to eliminate this problem. But even with these precautions, sometimes staining will result, so check periodically to be sure. Or to avoid any risk of stain, you can of course water plants at the sink.

This small- to medium-sized group of plants (to 30 inches) includes many varieties. Because they will not receive too much light, you must use plants that can survive low light levels. Bromeliads, the many peperomias and pileas, and African violets are all suitable table plants. Here is a list of plants to try for tables and desks:

African violets (many)
Aechmea chantinii
Agave victoriae reginae
Aloe aristata
Ananas cosmosus (pineapple plant)
Asplenium nidus (bird's-nest fern)
A. viviparum
Begonia erthrophylla (beefsteak begonia)
B. luxurians
B. paulensis
Beaucarnea recurvata (ponytail plant)
Cordyline terminalis (ti plant)
Dracaena deremsis warnecki
D. godseffiana
Episcias
Fittonia verschaffeltii
Guzmania lingulata

G. monostachia
Haworthia fasciata
H. margaritifera
Kalanchoe beharensis
K. blossfeldiana
Neoregelia carolinae
Peperomia (many varieties)
Pilea (many varieties)
Philodendron soderoi
Spathiphyllum clevelandii
Scindapsus aureus (pothos)
Syngonium podophyllum (nephthytis)
Tradescantia zebrina (wandering jew)

Episcias make lovely table or desk plants, neither too large nor too small and relatively undemanding in light requirements. (Photo by Matthew Barr)

*A window garden of assorted houseplants, citrus (left),
poinsettia (right), help to make cold winters warming inside.
(Photo courtesy Brock Arms)*

WINDOW PLANTS

The window garden as a decorative element serves its purpose. It brings fresh green into the room and provides a cheerful atmosphere, and it can also act as drapery to give you privacy. However, too often window plants look unkempt, with leaves pushing against the glass. Thus select plants that are upright growers or low bushy ones rather than branching and sprawling types.

There is a wide array of plants to use for windows (where there is generally good light). However, most sills cannot accommodate any plant in a container more than 8 inches in diameter (even with shelving). Instead of using different pots at windows, try to unify the garden with one type: plastic white ones or terra cotta. Too many different pots create a spotty effect that ruins the beauty of the window garden. Group large plants at bottom shelves or sill, with the smaller ones at top (if you are using shelves). Always be sure to allow growing space for plants. And remember that too many plants make the window garden a jungle and prevent light from entering the room, and too few plants look sparse and do not provide sufficient eye appeal.

Here are some small- and medium-sized plants, generally from 10 to 30 inches tall, for window gardens:

Aglaonema commutatum (Chinese evergreen)
Alocasia watsoniana
Begonia erthrophylla (beefsteak begonia)
B. paulensis
Coleus varieties
Dieffenbachia amoena (dumbcane)
D. bowmannii
D. hoffmannii
Dracaena sanderiana

Haemanthus coccineus (blood lily)
Hoffmannia roezlii
Maranta leuconeura kerchoveana (prayer plant)
Philodendron andreanum
P. pertusum (Swiss cheese plant)
P. verrucosum
Sansevieria trifasciata (snake plant)

*This lovely window garden is a conglomerate of many plants—
among them ferns, grape ivy, citrus, angel and rex begonia. The
natural feeling of the outdoors which this garden suggests blends
well with the rustic colonial furnishings of the room to create a
unified picture. (Photo by Molly Adams)*

*A lacy davallia fern on a pedestal and philodendrons greet visitors
to this home. The massive dieffenbachia and philodendrons
balance the heavy pedestal, and together with the smaller plant
on the table* (Asparagus sprengeri) *help to create a setting of
inviting greenery in a small corner. (Photo by Matthew Barr)*

PEDESTAL PLANTS

Pedestal plants come in 12- to 16-inch containers. They are not as large as tree-type plants or as small as window plants but fall somewhere between the two categories. These rather large plants include many fine begonias, cacti, and succulents, and lovely ferns.

The advantage of the pedestal is that it elevates the plant, putting it on display. And the pedestal and plant can be moved; if you do not like them in one area, try them in another place. Also, the pedestal-plant combination saves buying more expensive tree-type plants and yet can serve the same purpose to provide vertical area.

For pedestals use compact growers or semitrailing plants; branching plants will obstruct traffic. Keep plants well groomed because they are always on display. Here is a selection of plants for pedestals:

Aglaonema commutatum (Chinese evergreen)
Aspidistra elatior (cast-iron plant)
Beaucarnea recurvata (ponytail plant)
Begonia imperialis 'Otto Forster'
B. luxurians
B. 'Ricky Minter'
Blechnum brasiliense
Codiaeum (croton)
Crassula argentea (jade tree)
Dracaena sanderiana
Echinocactus grusonii (golden barrel cactus)
Euphorbia grandicornis
Neoregelia carolinae
Nephrolepis exaltata (many varieties) (Boston fern)
Philodendron panduraeforme
P. wendlendii
Woodwardia orientalis (chain fern)

FLOOR PLANTS

These are the large plants that serve several purposes in a room. They are design elements, and whether used in a corner or against a window wall they make impressive statements. A pyramidal and vertical plant like *Araucaria excelsa*, the Norfolk pine, is handsome in a corner. Palms with canopies of green fronds are other good floor or tree-type plants, but be wary because, of the many palms, only a few are symmetrical and suitable for corners. And do not overlook flowering plants like camellias, large bromeliads, or even tall orchids. (If the floor plant you select is not as tall as it appeared in the store and does not fill the desired area, put it on a plant pedestal.)

Pastel walls are an excellent background for floor plants, making them dramatic showpieces. Every leaf is prominent, and the trunks and stems are beautifully silhouetted. A wall provides space for branching habit, and the plant looks like sculpture. Against walls use branching and "weeping" plants or, for stark beauty, a cactus.

When placing plants against walls, never cram them in; allow some space behind them. If plants are against walls with no windows, do supply artificial light (outlined in Chapter 7). Be sure to plan ahead for ceiling track and fixtures to accommodate lights because no plant will live long without some source of light. Floor plants are usually in 20-inch diameter pots. Suitable containers in keeping with the character of the room must be chosen (see Chapter 8). Here is a sampling of the many tree-type floor plants (hanging and trailing plants are included in Chapter 6):

Agave americana marginata (century plant)
Araucaria excelsa (Norfolk pine)
Caryota mitis (fishtail palm)
Chamaedorea elegans bella (parlor palm)
C. erumpens (bamboo palm)

Table and desk plants are used in conjunction with floor plants to create a warm feeling in this handsome interior. Two dracaenas, not usually thought of as "pedestal" plants, are used here for their height and greenery against the expanse of wood wall. The large fern at right softens the effect of the wood legs of the table and pedestals, while the dieffenbachia in the corner adds natural color while hiding an air duct opening. A small plant of ivy on the desk completes the setting. (Bradley Little, Designer)

Here a tall cordyline is used to frame an entrance, yet it is part
of the room and provides needed vertical accent. (John Hall,
Designer)

Chrysalidocarpus (Areca) lutescens (butterfly palm)
Citrus (many kinds)
Cereus peruvianus
Clusia rosea
Cocos weddelliana
Cycads (many species)
Dieffenbachia exotica
Dracaena fragrans massangeana (corn plant)
D. marginata
Ficus benjamina
F. carica (common fig)
F. elastica (rubber tree)
F. lyrata (fiddleleaf fig)
Howea forsteriana (kentia palm)
Lemairocereus marginatus
L. thurberi
Lophocereus schottii
Pandanus veitchii (screw pine)
Philodendron bipinnatifidum
P. selloum (fingerleaf philodendron)
P. squamiferum
Phoenix roebelenii (miniature date palm)
Podocarpus macrophylla
P. nagi
Polyscias fruticosa (ming tree)
Rhapis excelsa (lady palm)
Schefflera (Brassaia) actinophylla (umbrella tree)
Trichocereus spachianus
Veitchia mereli
Vriesea fenestralis
Yucca aloifolia (Spanish dagger)

In spite of the many things to see and enjoy in this room, the addition of a vertical plant (cordyline), with horizontal components, makes one feel it is a home and not a setting. (Cruthers Conway, Designer)

In this window garden all kinds of plants are grown; they are small or medium specimens and include wee ferns, episcias, cordyline, pilea, and, at upper left, cissus (grape ivy). (Photo by Matthew Barr)

4 🍃

The Garden at Home

In recent years the importance of live plants as part of interiors has gone beyond the single specimen or decorative accent tree or large plant. In some areas groups of plants are being used to become part of the total room: to line windows, to fill a corner. Display planting of this kind requires careful choice of plants or an unruly jungle effect results, which is hardly in keeping with good design.

Atriums—central courts filled with plants—are another part of indoor gardening. These special places are becoming more popular, as are garden rooms adjacent to the living part of the home, where they become exciting extensions of the house. Dining rooms, living rooms, halls, entryways, kitchens are all places for plants today.

GENERAL HINTS

Years ago window plants were part of most homes. The window garden still has its uses, but its placement and the plants used should be given careful consideration. Too often a few plants at the window look just like that—a few plants at the window. There is little harmony, scale, or proportion involved, and the results generally look like a tacked-on afterthought as far as total design is concerned.

In addition, window plants demand special consideration. The floor in the area must be impervious to water, the sills must be protected, and the plants must be shaded from hot summer sun. This is more work than perhaps is wanted by the busy indoor gardener. However, plants at windows are still necessary in many situations, so mix and match them with care, just as you would design your outdoor garden.

There is also a difference between a window garden in a kitchen or bathroom and in a living or dining room. The kitchen garden can be a casual conglomeration of leafy beauties and flowering plants like African violets. In the living part of the home, however, the plants must be more sophisticated; better species and mature plants are needed to be harmonious with the appointments. Vertical and horizontal line must be considered, and there should be a combination of bushy and columnar plants. Avoid rampant growers and pendant plants, which do better when placed in baskets in the air. At windows fronds and branches are thwarted and plants rarely look good.

Rather than placing plants directly on the window sill, it is sometimes better to have galvanized trays made to fit specific areas on the floor. In this way the plants become part of the room and can be seen, especially where there are floor-to-ceiling windows and no sills. Fill the tray with gravel, and place pots and plants on the gravel bed so they can benefit from the excess moisture that drains from pots.

For the kitchen select medium-sized plants such as kohlerias, co-

In an entry hall, the guest is welcomed by a planter greenery; a unique way to use plants, but care must be taken to provide sufficient artificial light. Plants are small ferns and philodendrons, with a large palm at right. (Raul Coronel, Designer)

lumneas, and African violets. In the living room use some tall plants, to 48 inches (mature *Medinilla magnifica* or a treelike philodendron make a fine statement). Mix tall and low plants as you would in a garden to create a total scene that harmonizes with the room rather than a potpourri of plants that mean little as a unified grouping. Remember that these plants are always on display, unlike kitchen plants that visitors generally do not see.

HALLS AND ENTRYWAYS

Your entrance hall is where people get the first impression of your home. Many times these areas have little or no natural light, so choosing plants that can tolerate low light levels is the key to success. If the space is large enough, try a plant on a pedestal. For tables, shelves, and benches, concentrate on plants that can tolerate shady situations, such as cissus and sansevierias.

If there is no room for furniture in the hall or entryway, a plant may be your only answer to providing some decoration. Use tall vertical specimens that do not take up too much space. Try a leafy bold philodendron or a tall false aralia (Dizygotheca).

Other good locations for somewhat tall plants are the foot of an open stairway or a stairwell. The plants serve two purposes: decoration for the space as well as handsome viewing from the stairs.

In halls without any natural light you might want to use a decorator's trick: Rotate plants between the living room and hall. This is easy if pots are on casters; you roll them to a new location.

Above all, in halls and entryways do not forget cascading plants. They are impressive on tall tables or shelves, where pendant leaves can cover somewhat straight lines or furniture hardware. Use appropriate mats and saucers so water stain does not become a problem on furniture tops.

Finally, do not forget the small bouquet of fresh flowers in hall areas. This is a fine way to say welcome to guests.

LIVING ROOMS

No matter how small your living room may be, there is always a place for plants. Indeed, the smaller the area the more likely plants will help the space esthetically and functionally. In large living rooms plants will provide dimension and charm and avoid a display hall setting.

Study your living room space carefully, preferably before furniture is in it, before selecting plants. Think of plants in terms of shape (as explained in Chapter 2) to determine just where they might serve a decorative effect, like a picture on the wall or to substitute for an end table or as a means to guide traffic through a room.

Most living rooms are good-sized, so select large plants rather than tiny ones that will be out of scale. If the space is long and narrow, choose an upright plant with slender branches such as false aralia (Dizygotheca). If there is more space and you need some drama, try *Dracaena marginata* or *Ficus benjamina*, branching plants that make a bold statement. If it is a contemporary or modern interior, think about large cacti, because they are visually striking in such settings.

If the room is small, plants with leaves of similar value and color to the walls will make the room appear larger. For example, a cascading variegated spider plant against an off-white wall.

Plants are ideal for large window walls to break the monotony of the span or plants may act as a frame for a fireplace. Other places for plants are behind a pair of chairs and table, where they supply necessary vertical height and complete the setting.

Be courageous in your use of plants and do something different. For example, instead of a long table behind a sofa try a row of identical plants. Use broad-leaved species to create a mass which will relate to the

*There is a wealth of good plant material put to good use in this
living room. The fireplace wall remains clear and uncluttered
with the plants serving as pictures on either side.* Ficus lyrata
at left; Dracaena massangeana, *right. The lovely group of plants
(left front) is* Dracaena warnecki, *a splendid indoor low light
subject. (Harold Leavitt, Architect)* ABOVE

*This charming traditional living room has plants that are in scale
with the room while at the same time help to make the room seem
larger. The* Ficus lyrata *at the right with large leaves appears
close to the viewer while the fine foliage of the palm seems far
away. Note that plants are near windows to give them sufficient
light. (Cruthers Conway, Designer)* RIGHT

sofa. To create an illusion of space use plant groupings toward the middle of the room (do not however, block traffic flow). And do not rule out plants where floor space is limited. Consider the appeal of lovely hanging baskets of filmy ferns and tropical trailers. When using hanging plants, try three at different heights for an impressive display.

Once the large plants are in place, use a few complementary table or desk plants to pull it all together. Do not make the living room a plant shop, but do try to balance the treelike specimens with smaller pot plants placed strategically throughout the room (they can be moved at times to change the character of the space).

BEDROOMS

Most people do not like plants in bedrooms; I think they have a psychological thing about the plants robbing the air of the oxygen needed to breathe. (Actually, just the opposite is true because plants give off oxygen during the day.) Plants do more than make a bedroom look nice; they impart a soft, relaxing character to the room. Graceful palms or ferns on tables or floors are airy and appealing. They can make going to bed calming and waking up cheerful.

In the past, small plants were used on dressers or chests of drawers. Today's bedroom is more designed for living than just sleeping so let your imagination go. If you are an avid gardener this is the place to have many plants, because it is your private place. Be brave and try a pair of arching palms to frame a headboard or have baskets of plants in tandem to form a column of green that acts as a screen. Many bedrooms are divided into areas of sleeping, dressing, and sitting spaces. Plants can be used as dividers or screens to provide a sense of privacy.

Keep the watering can in the nearby bathroom so you will not forget to water plants.

This handsome room uses hanging plants and floor plants to blend with the natural brick walls and at the window and table (front) are chlorophytums, in the corner a tall schefflera that provides vertical accent. (Hedrich Blessing photo; Don Konl, Designer)

An acrylic pedestal holds a lovely cascading grape ivy; the lush green adds color and texture to the neutral corner and balances with the palm at left. (Richard Kent, Designer)

BATHROOMS

The bathroom is an overlooked room of the house for plants, and yet, ironically, here is where plants will grow the best. Humidity from your daily shower, and the warmth of the bathroom are all conducive to making plants grow well, and plants distract from the sterile fixtures of the bathroom. Also, frosted glass in bathroom windows is an advantage for plant growth because it provides diffused light, not too bright, not too dark, which is exactly what most plants prefer.

Floor plants are often out of the question here because space may be limited but baskets of ferns and hanging plants in wall brackets can be most suitable. There are many plants that will prosper in the bathroom: fittonias, marantas, anthuriums, and even orchids! On vanities, shelves, or in hanging baskets, there are innumerable places for small- to medium-sized pot plants. Use distinctive pots to complement the decor, and try all kinds of plants; you will be surprised at how well they will grow.

If the bathroom is without windows, try some plants under fluorescent lights on a shelf or table, or use ceiling spotlights for convenience. Do not overlook the possibility of placing plants adjacent to mirrors to create a double reflection so two plants appear as four.

If the shower area is light and spacious consider a tropical floating garden with plants in ornamental containers. This is highly effective. In summary, do not let the bathroom be bare; by all means try to incorporate some plants into its design.

KITCHENS

Today's kitchens are a far cry from the large kitchens of yesteryear (although the tendency lately is for bigger kitchens). A personal touch is needed in the kitchen, and plants are the answer. Furthermore, since you

This lovely *Areca* palm is just the right green note to this
handsome bathroom. Without it, the room appeared bare, almost
sterile. (Benham Interiors)   ABOVE

This elegant bathroom is well landscaped with plants. Several
ferns are in the pedestal at right and a cascading grape ivy hangs
at left. For balance and additional interest, smaller plants are
placed around the bathtub. (Cardan Interiors)   BELOW

*A lovely and inviting kitchen window sill is gaily bedecked with
African violets. Swedish ivy is the trailing plant above the
window. (Paul DuPont, Designer)*

spend a great deal of time in the kitchen, you will want cheerful, colorful plants to brighten gray days. No matter how small the kitchen is, there are herbs, flowering plants, and even creepers and mosses that can thrive and enliven the room.

Shelves, cabinet tops, and window sills are all prime spots for kitchen plants. Such popular flowering plants as African violets, geraniums, and miniature begonias grow luxuriantly because most kitchens have better humidity than other rooms in the home. Cooking and water running add to the amount of moisture in the air.

As mentioned, herbs are attractive kitchen plants and provide wonderful fresh flavorings for cooking. You can grow basil, chives, rosemary, sage, and thyme in small pots at kitchen windows. There are dozens of medium-sized plants that will also prosper at windows, including pileas, peperomias, marantas, ruellias, and syngoniums. Floor plants may be out of the question in the average kitchen, but if there is some space, try a small rhapis palm, a cycad, or even some trailing begonias.

Some kitchens are white or yellow, and apple-green or variegated plants look splendid in such situations, but remember to use appropriate pots. Choose one color rather than different ones that can clash with color schemes. Today, many kitchens also include the dining area and if you need some type of partition to separate the areas, a few tall plants are a perfect answer.

DINING ROOMS

Most dining rooms are small; even so, plants are desirable when properly chosen and well placed. Select small- or medium-sized plants; avoid towering ones. There is something infinitely appealing about eating surrounded by lush greenery. So even if you think your dining area is too small for plants, think again.

In this room three plants provide warmth and color. Placement is perfect with an aglaonema on the table, a palm behind it in the corner, and on the shelf grape ivy. The result is an excellent balance of mass and color. (Hepple, Designer)

Without a sofa to create mass, dining rooms with their tabletop create a secondary plane, and plants are useful in rescuing an awkward situation. Also, many times the dining room is apt to appear like a forest of table legs and chair legs. Do bring in low masses of grouped plants to create a balance, or tall leafy plants for vertical contrast.

Corners are fine places for a towering palm, a schefflera, or even a cactus. Near windows, consider smaller plants (more in scale with dining rooms) such as *Dracaena massangeana* or *D. sanderiana*. For added impact use a few pots of flowering plants like clivias and amaryllis to accompany sideboards and buffets, perhaps. Geraniums, too, can be brought in as seasonal color to brighten dining rooms.

If the room is small, avoid hanging baskets at the perimeter of the room because they may hinder traffic, and bumping accidentally into a pot plant is no great joy.

SPECIAL ROOMS

RECREATION ROOMS

This area is generally large to accommodate many family activities and often it is used as an auxiliary place for entertaining guests, so you want it to be as charming and pleasant as possible. The recreation room usually has many windows, so there is ample space for plants, and high ceilings can accommodate very large ones.

Vinyl and tile and indoor/outdoor carpeting are often used in these areas because they are durable and can take abuse. This is ideal for plants because there is never any problem with water stains from plants; a mop takes up excess water quickly.

Because the recreation room is used so much for entertaining, the surroundings should be as cheerful as possible. Plants definitely provide much of this pleasantness. Almost any living room plant will be suitable, but try to incorporate at least one or two tree-type plants to give the room some character. Look around the room and decide just where the plants will best fit into the setting. For example, one large ficus in a corner with a pedestal plant such as a rhizomatous begonia near a window along with smaller table or desk plants to balance the greenery may be all that is necessary. Any shelving is a fine place for small trailing plants such as plectranthus and chlorophytum and upright growers like African violets.

ATRIUMS

The atrium is most prevalent in California but is also popular in other climates and deserves some thought for places for plants because it is an excellent plan. It is valuable as a greenery because in many areas open land is at a premium; the atrium provides a garden within the home.

The atrium garden gives complete privacy, has good light for plants, and when roofed over (in untemperate climates) actually becomes a small conservatory. The room is generally rectangular or square, with a tile or quarry floor. Because the atrium is a part of the total plan of the house, again, select plants as though they were pieces of furniture; they will be just as important in the overall design. This is the place for specimen plants and those grown in tree form (standards) such as roses and fuchsias. Use ornamental pots to show off plants properly rather than planting directly in the ground.

Look for vertical and horizontal accent; this is not a place for bushy sprawling plants. All plants should be well trimmed and beautifully shaped. Use small-leaved foliage along with bold-leaved plants to create harmony, and repeat patterns and materials and plants for balance. Also remember that you will cross this area to get to other rooms in the house, so leave enough space for walking. Where doors enter onto the atrium,

This garden-recreation room off the patio invites the guest at once with its array of colorful plants. At the far left is Ficus benjamina. *The basket plants are lush plectranthus and on the floor beneath them some cyclamen. And a very fine African violet is on the glass table.*

*A clever use of plants is shown here defining two separate
rooms. At the same time the area serves as a walk-through garden.
The accent plants in the center are crotons and a pair of palms
flank the entrance to the other room.*

use the same type plants indoors at the entrance and repeat them in the atrium to create a flow of color.

GARDEN ROOMS

These special rooms for plants and guests are favorites of mine, and I have designed and built four different, attractive garden rooms for four different houses. (See color photo.) I think a garden room is truly a gardener's dream because here you can grow almost any kind of plant, flowering and foliage, with considerable success. In addition, the garden room will become the focal point of a well-designed house, and adjacent to a living or dining room it becomes an extension of the house.

The garden room can be many things, but for simplicity we can say it should have the following points:

A floor impervious to water
A ceiling that admits 40 percent natural light
Adequate ventilation
Electrical outlets
Water outlets
Places for furniture
Floor-drainage facilities

You can grow almost any kind of plant in a garden room; there are few restrictions. Large foliage plants such as schefflera and palms can mix with flowering gems such as orchids and bromeliads. Smaller pot plants can complement the setting to make a living greenery that your family and guests will love.

Mr. Kramer's garden room has an array of plants: ferns, orchids, begonias. It is a light, bright, and airy room, a festival of greenery used as the entrance to the house. (Morley Baer photo; Andrew R. Addkison, Designer)

5 🌿

Plant Lists and Descriptions

The plants in the following list are not the only ones for indoor decoration. There are many more. However, these were chosen for special characteristics such as color or shape or because the plants are easy to grow. Appropriate cultural notes are given with descriptions.

Abutilon hybrids. To 48 inches. Spotted green leaves, rangy growth; bell flowers. Good for one season only, but very colorful; needs plenty of water.

Adiantum cuneatum (delta maidenhair). To 20 inches. Dark green; feathery and branching. Give moist shady conditions.

A. hispidulum. To 12 inches. Forked leaves; branching. Moist shady conditions.

A. tenurum wrightii. To 20 inches. Pale green; dainty fronds. Moist shady conditions.

Aechmea chantinii. To 40 inches. A bromeliad with leathery, vase-shaped leaves. Elegant addition to a room and grows with almost no care.

Aeschynanthus speciosus (lipstick vine). A trailer, to 48 inches, with oval dark green leaves and red flowers. Lush and bold; needs good light and even moisture.

African violets. Generally small, with rosette growth and colorful bloom.

Agave americana marginata (century plant). To 5 feet. A giant, with serrated leaves that are green margined with white. Water; allow to dry out before watering again.

A. victoriae reginae. To 10 inches. Rosette of narrow olive-green leaves penciled white; a compact globe. Keep somewhat dry.

Aglaonema commutatum (Chinese evergreen). To 2 feet. Bright silver markings on dark green leaves; generally a single trunk. Fountain or rosette erect growth. Will tolerate dimmest corner.

Alocasia watsoniana. To 28 inches. Silver veins on corrugated blue-green leaves; exotic. Needs high humidity and bright light to prosper.

Aloe aristata. To 10 inches. A green-gray rosette; leaves with marginal teeth. Grows easily with routine care.

Araucaria excelsa (Norfolk pine). To 48 inches. Looks like a miniature Christmas tree. Very erect; branching and vertical. Keep somewhat dry, out of sun.

Asparagus sprengeri (emerald fern). To 48 inches. A feathery, needlelike, emerald-green plant. Needs plenty of water.

Aspidistra elatior (cast-iron plant). To 30 inches. Shiny green-black leaves, clustered and upright. A plant for the most untenable situation.

Asplenium nidus (bird's-nest fern). To 30 inches. A rosette of apple-green leaves. Temperamental; doesn't like it too dry or too moist.

A. viviparum. To 30 inches. A filmy fern. A shade lover.

Bambusa (bamboo). Many species, and several make excellent houseplants growing to great heights.

Beaucarnea recurvata (ponytail plant). Narrow leaves in cascade fashion; good table plant. Hardy, easy-to-grow houseplant.

Begonia (angel wing). To 36 inches. Angel-wing-shaped leaves and bowers of flowers. Give some sun.

B. 'Cleopatra'. To 20 inches. Star-shaped leaves splashed gold, brown, and chartreuse. Needs plenty of water; bright light.

B. 'Elsie M. Frey'. Another good trailing plant. Bright light.

B. erthrophylla (beefsteak begonia). To 14 inches. Crested round green leaves; good table plant. Will tolerate shade.

B. imperialis 'Otto Forster'. To 28 inches. Dark green leaves and white flowers. Give good light.

B. limminghiana. One of the finest cascading plants available. Give good light and even moisture.

B. luxurians. Looks like a tiny palm. Fine houseplant.

B. paulenis. Large quilted leaves with pale veins. Likes moisture and humidity.

B. 'Ricky Minter'. To 36 inches. Large bright green leaves; splendid pedestal plant.

B. 'Shippy's Garland'. To 40 inches. A bower of green; trailing.

B. 'Skeezar'. To 30 inches. A cascade of green; trailing.

Billbergia venezueleana. To 48 inches. Vase-shaped, leathery-leaved plant. Good pedestal plant. Grows in most adverse conditions.

Blechnum brasiliense. To 48 inches. Coarse fronds branching from central trunk. Good as a floor plant. Water, allow to dry out before watering again.

Calathea makoyana. To 40 inches. Olive green–pink leaves veined silver. Good for a table. Likes good moisture and humidity.

Campanula isophylla. A trailer, with small green leaves and white flowers. Likes coolness (50° F) at night.

Caryota mitis (fishtail palm). To 72 inches. A branching and dramatic palm. Good floor plant. Keep somewhat dry.

Chamaedorea erumpens (bamboo palm). To 72 inches. Fine branching dark green palm. Give plenty of water.

C. elegans bella (parlor palm). To 60 inches. Dark green fronds. More bushy than most palms. Give plenty of water.

Chlorophytum elatum (spider plant). A favorite trailer, with arching grasslike green leaves. Likes even moisture.

Chrysalidocarpus (Areca) lutescens (butterfly palm). To 40 inches. Widely branching graceful palm. Don't overwater.

Chysis laevis. A trailing orchid with papery thin leaves and waxy orange flowers in sprigs. Keep dry for several weeks after blooming.

Cibotium menziesii (Mexican tree fern). Lovely graceful fern with stout trunk and emerald-green fronds.

Cissus rhombifolia (grape ivy). A trailer to 48 inches. Favorite basket plant; dark green scalloped leaves. Fine for shady areas.

Citrus. Many kinds. Deep green leathery leaves. Good in tubs for floor plants. Need bright light, good moisture.

Clusia rosea. To 60 inches. Dark green round leaves; erect growth habit. Keep evenly moist.

Coleus. Good as trailers in baskets. Takes buckets of water.

Codiaeum (croton). Enormous array of different colored hybrids. Need buckets of water and sun.

Columnea arguta. Trailer; dainty pointed leaves. Prefers shady humid conditions.

Cordyline terminalis (ti plant). To 60 inches. Deep green leaves edged red in fountain shape. Good window plant. Grows readily in most situations. Mature plants can be trained to grow in treelike shape.

Crassula argentea (jade tree). To 40 inches. A succulent, with round green leathery leaves and a central trunk. Don't overwater.

Cryptanthus. Many varieties. To 14 inches. Leaves in many colors. Don't overwater.

Cycads. Many kinds, all good. Resemble palms, and make fine table or pedestal plants. Keep somewhat dry.

Davallia fejeenis (rabbit's-foot fern). Fifteen-inch fronds. Dainty fluffy-leaved plant. Needs filtered light, coolness.

Dendrobium pierardii. Three-inch pink blooms in March or April. Easy to grow. Rest for several weeks after bloom.

Dieffenbachia amoena (dumbcane). To 36 inches. Green and white large-leaved plant. Keep evenly moist.

D. bowmannii. To 36 inches. Chartreuse-mottled green foliage. Keep evenly moist.

D. exotica. To 48 inches. Narrow habit with green and white mottled leaves.

D. hoffmannii. To 36 inches. Oblong pointed satiny green leaves, marbled white.

D. splendens. To 36 inches. Velvety green foliage and white dots.

Dipladenia amoena (Mexican love vine). Dark green oblong leaves; pink flowers. Needs plenty of sun.

Dracaena deremsis warnecki. Striped green-and-white beauty. Keep evenly moist.

D. fragrans massangeana (corn plant). Arching yellow and green 24-inch leaves. Likes moisture.

D. godseffiana. Yellow and green 6-inch leaves.

D. marginata. Eighteen-inch dark green leaves edged red. Likes a somewhat dry soil.

D. sanderiana. Nine-inch green leaves banded white. Prefers good moisture.

Episcia. Trailers; exotic foliage and brilliant flowers in spring and summer. Needs high humidity and heat.

Euphorbia grandicornis. To 48 inches. Bizarre but beautiful branched knobby plant. Keep dry.

Fatsia japonica. To 5 feet. Leathery lobed dark green leaves. Nice branching habit. Likes coolness.

Ficus benjamina (banyan tree). To 5 feet. Dense head of gracefully drooping branches. Let dry out between waterings.

F. carica (common fig). To 4 feet. Large green leaves. Needs even moisture.

F. elastica decora. To 5 feet. Thick glossy green leaves. Keep evenly moist.

F. lyrata (fiddleleaf fig). To 5 feet. Enormous leaves; avoid drafts. Keep evenly moist.

Fittonia vershaffeltii. Dense creepers; leaves with red veins. Needs high humidity; no sun.

Guzmania lingulata. Twenty-six-inch rosette of apple-green leaves. Grows anywhere.

G. monostachia. Twenty-six-inch rosette with red, black, and white flower head. Grows easily with little care.

Gynura aurantiaca (velvet plant). To 30 inches. Large purple leaves. Likes even moisture.

Haemanthus coccineus (blood lily). To 10 inches. Spectacular red flowers.

Haworthia fasciata. Small erect rosette; small dark green incurved leaves banded with white. Prefers dry soil.

H. margaritifera. Low-growing rosettes with pointed leaves with white granules; dense sprays of flowers. Keep somewhat dry.

Hoffmannia roezlii. To 30 inches. Copper-brown and bronze foliage. Keep evenly moist.

Howea forsteriana (kentia palm). To 5 feet. Broad, hanging, and waxy dark green fronds. Give plenty of water in summer, not so much the rest of the year.

Hoya carnosa (wax plant). To 4 feet. White flowers with pink centers. Grow somewhat dry.

Kalanchoe beharensis. To 4 feet. Large petaled leaves. Somewhat temperamental. Likes good moisture.

K. blossfeldiana. To 30 inches. Plants vary in type of growth and foliage. Fleshy green leaves; clusters of small, showy red or orange blossoms. Seasonal plant.

K. tomentosa. To 20 inches. Brown-spotted gray-green fuzzy leaves.

Maranta leuconeura kerchoveana (prayer plant). To 15 inches. Oval glaucous leaves, pale grayish green, with rows of brown and dark green spots. Likes good humidity and moisture.

Medinella magnifica. To 4 feet. Lush dark green plant with splendid flowers. Likes warmth.

Neoregelia carolinae. Dark green leaves; flowers are insignificant. Grows easily with little care.

Nephrolepis exaltata (Boston fern). Fronds to 5 feet. Bushy. Keep shady and moist.

Pandanus veitchii (screw pine). Variegated recurved leaves. Water, allow to dry before watering again.

Peperomia. Smooth-edged leaves and insignificant flowers; many have vining growth. Small amenable plants.

Philodendron andreanum. To 36 inches. Dark green leaves; vine. Needs good heat and humidity.

P. bipinnatifidum. To 30 inches. Dark green scalloped leaves; dramatic vine. Give moist shady spot.

P. oxycardium. To 36 inches. Heart-shaped leaves; vine. Grows easily.

P. panduraeforme. To 40 inches. Dark green lance-shaped leaves.

P. pertusum (Swiss cheese plant). To 40 inches. Large cut-leaves. Keep evenly moist.

P. selloum (fingerleaf philodendron). To 30 inches. Notched leaves; rosette. Keep somewhat moist.

P. soderoi. To 40 inches. Lovely heart-shaped dark green, veined leaves. Likes good moisture and humidity.

P. squamiferum. To 60 inches. Rich, green lobed leaves; vine. Likes good moisture and humidity.

P. verrucosum. To 24 inches. Multicolored heart-shaped leaves; vine. Unusual philodendron.

P. wendlandii. Twenty-six-inch rosette; lush green foliage. Keep evenly moist.

Phoenix roebelenii (miniature date palm). To about 40 inches. Thick crowns of dark green leaves. Keep moist in summer, somewhat dry in winter.

Pilea. Plain or variegated leaves; clusters of tiny flowers. Grows easily.

Plectranthus coleoides (Swedish ivy). To 20 inches. Small crinkled leaves; white-and-purple blooms. Likes plenty of water.

Podocarpus macrophylla maki. To 48 inches. Erect, branching, waxy black and green leaves. Likes coolness.

P. nagi. Spreading, shining green foliage. Likes coolness.

Polyscias fruticosa (ming tree). To 60 inches. Fine tiny-leaved plant; central trunk. Keep evenly moist.

Polypodium polycarpon (hare's-foot fern). To 30 inches. Yellow-green fronds; robust. Grows best on slab.

Rhapsis excelsa (lady palm). To 48 inches. Lush bamboo-type growth. Likes coolness; no sun.

Sansevieria trifasciata (snake plant). To 30 inches. Lance leaves with yellow bands. Grows in any situation.

Saxifraga sarmentosa (strawberry geranium). To 20 inches. Coarsely toothed reddish leaves veined white; white flowers. Grows in any situation.

Schefflera (Brassaia) actinophylla (umbrella tree). To 72 inches. Tall branching plant, large leaves. Dry out between waterings.

*Palms are used with flourish in this handsome room; they are in
exquisite urns and the heavy mass feeling balances the light, airy
character of the iron furniture. The ivy espalier effect against
window walls is unique; note slats to allow natural light above
(Larry Mulscher, Designer)*

A garden room is a place for plants and a place to sit and enjoy them. Orchids, ferns, and palms are a few of the many plants grown in this inviting setting. (Matthew Barr photo; Andrew R. Addkison, Designer)

Off a dining room this lovely garden room houses many tropical plants and provides a beautiful view as well. Inside, bougainvillaea climbs the posts of this garden room and orchids and bromeliads deck the wall shelves. The ceiling is part glass and part fabric-covered plywood. (Photo by Joyce R. Wilson; Andrew R. Addkison, Designer)

Palms, pandanus, and assorted houseplants decorate this corner behind a sofa providing color and a pleasing scene. Against the shutters the plants appear silhouetted, adding to the drama. (Matthew Barr photo; Andrew R. Addkison, Designer)

The date palm near the window walls is a dramatic element in this room and makes a fine vertical statement. The light green of the table fern continues the green of the sofa pillows. (Daisy Cresson, Designer)

A high-ceilinged room needs a tall plant and the schefflera with its canopy shape is perfect here. On the pedestal in the corner is a fine specimen philodendron providing a solid block of green. (Michael Morrison, Designer)

An exquisite urn holds a specimen Philodendron radiantum *flanked by floor ferns to bring color and interest to an otherwise unusable space. Ceiling lights under the staircase allow these luxuriant plants to flourish in this lightless corner. (J. A. Perkins, Designer)*

Philodendrons make excellent houseplants where there is little light. Here P. hastatum *provides vertical thrust and green accent, while the fern in the pedestal balances the greenery. (Est Est Design)*

*An unusual arrangement of ivy in the candle chandelier brings
the outdoors indoors in this room corner setting; a lush fern
provides deep green color at the corner. (Peter Shore, Designer)*

A bromeliad, Neoregelia carolinae, *is the coffee table accent; it
is small and in scale with the room.* Dracaena marginata *on a
pedestal graces the window and breaks the strong vertical lines
of the draperies. (Bill Benner, Designer)*

*The ficus tree is branching and airy and just the right vertical
influence this high-ceilinged room needs. Table plants bring color
forward as well as to the rear of the room, causing the eye to
move easily from place to place. (Ron Collier, Interior Designer)*

This charming greenery is at the edge of a fireplace and gives the area needed color, bright and cheerful. Only three plants are used—African violets and cissus—and yet the setting is lovely. The plants must of course be removed when the fireplace is in use. (Joyce R. Wilson photo)

A bathroom that is a tropical paradise with all kinds of greenery that act as a frame for the tub. The total result is appealing and infinitely charming. (Laurena Hepple, Designer)

Scindapsus aureus (pothos). Twelve-inch dark green leaves laced with yellow; good basket plant. Grows in any situation.

Sedum morganianum (burro's tail). To 36 inches. Trailing; blue-green foliage and yellow blooms. Grows in any situation.

Spathiphyllum clevelandii. Long shiny leaves and white flowers. Keep somewhat moist.

Syngonium podophyllum (nephthytis). Trailer, with 6-inch leaves. Grows easily.

Tolmiea menziesii (piggy-back plant). To 30 inches. Apple-green lobed leaves. Likes plenty of water.

Tradescantia fluminensis (wandering jew). Oval leaves, lush growth. Likes water.

Trichocereus. Many fine species; some grow to gigantic heights. Mainly columnar cacti that need little care.

Veitchia mereli. To 8 feet. Lovely palm with central trunk; arching fronds at top. Keep warm with good moisture.

Woodwardia orientalis (chain fern). Long drooping stiff fronds; good basket plant. Keep moist and shady.

Yucca aloifolia (Spanish dagger). To 48 inches. Lance leaves on central trunk. Keep somewhat dry between waterings.

Zebrina pendula (wandering jew). To 16 inches. Purple leaves with silver bands. Likes moisture.

6 🍂

Hanging Gardens

Cascading and rosette-type plants (for example, ferns) have become very popular in recent years, and the art of working with eye-level gardens has become an important part of indoor plant decoration. This kind of gardening has several advantages. It puts plants on display where they can be seen from all angles; it fills space that otherwise would be barren. Plants grow lavishly in such situations because they have abundant air circulation and room to grow; and, perhaps most importantly, plants can be used almost anywhere in a room and become a decorative accent, used much like a wall painting or picture.

For years the only kind of containers for basket gardens were old-

A large Boston fern helps put vertical accent into this high-ceilinged room. It is luxuriant and beautiful and full, and a perfect contrast for the sharp, angular lines of the room and the furniture. At the latticed window it receives excellent light. (Photo by Joyce R. Wilson; Andrew R. Addkison, Designer)

fashioned wire ones that had to be lined with moss, but today there is an array of decorative containers for trailing plants. And the problem of basket gardening—dripping water on floors—is gone too because attach-on saucers and other devices are now at suppliers.

ABOUT BASKET PLANTS

There is something infinitely beautiful about trailing plants that cascade over pot edges in a fountain of green. The graceful lines cannot be ignored, and as something different to complement a room setting, they are tough to beat. Also effective in baskets, although not true trailers, are plants such as bushy impatiens, a cloud of red flowers, or chrysanthemums, caladiums, and coleus, all brightly colored desirable plants in the right situation.

No matter what plant you use, where you hang it (midway between floor and ceiling) and how you hang it (hardware, and placement) must be considered. Avoid placing the plant too close to the ceiling; in average rooms this will make it look ill-placed, and people will have to strain their necks to see it. Generally, the top of the plant should be at least 24 inches from the ceiling. Select a plant that is in scale with other objects in the room. Large rooms will need large plants such as ferns or mature grape ivy; smaller rooms are more suitable to coleus or plectranthus.

The place for basket plants is generally near a window, where all that is needed is a single specimen. Against a window wall use three plants at varying heights spaced equal distance from each other for a stellar display. Do not use a single trailing plant in a corner unless you can have other greenery around it—a tall floor plant next to it, or somewhat large table plants to pull the whole scene together. For smaller rooms like kitchens and bathrooms, use small plants, but in living areas look for something spectacular. Try a Christmas cactus or a superlative fern in an ornamental hanging container.

CONTAINERS AND ACCESSORIES

There are numerous containers for trailing plants. You may use the pot as is or place it in another, more decorative housing. Because the bottom and sides of hanging pots are easily seen, do use handsome containers. Wicker and bamboo baskets of all kinds are very popular, as are the sleek and simple spun-aluminum pots. Wooden buckets and kegs and slatted wooden baskets are other possibilities. One-of-a-kind pottery is good because it always brings a natural note into interiors.

Hanging devices for containers include chains, ropes, raffia, wire, macramé, and ceiling fixtures, in many styles, from gilded screw-in S hooks to standard eyebolts. Use a suitable support because an 8-inch pot filled with soil weighs about 60 pounds—a formidable hazard if it ever slips from its moorings. And be wary of lightweight chains; use the old-fashioned heavy chain available in brass, black, or silver finish. I have found that most chains and monofilament wires are fine for supports, but raffia or ropes eventually become worn and soiled.

No matter what kind of container you use, be sure it has drainage holes so excess water can escape. Pots without drainage holes invariably lead to the death of the plant because soil in them becomes waterlogged and sour and thus harms the plant. Some containers, for example, plastic ones, have premolded saucers attached to catch dripping water. But for the clay pots you will have to buy special wire pot hangers that attach to clay saucers. Or you can use the pot-within-a-pot method as described earlier or a pot on a clay saucer in the container to solve the water-drip problem. The lip-type saucer is necessary for basket containers so the pot hanger can grasp its edges and keep the saucer in place under the pot.

When you drill holes for the eyehooks or S hooks, try to find the studs in the ceiling (there is an inexpensive gadget on the market called a studfinder). This way you will not have to worry about drilling into plaster or nonsupportive materials. Recently, pulley-type hanging containers that

A very lovely hanging begonia is Begonia 'Ellen Dee' and this one is grown to perfection. It can add beauty to almost any sunny room as a hanging plant. (Photo courtesy Mrs. Carl Meyer) ABOVE

Hanging ferns decorate this entryway. The mass of the palm beneath continues the flow of color to the floor. On the other side of the area is a palm to balance the setting Thus, two design elements are used here to equal an attractive whole. (Cardan Interiors) RIGHT

move up and down for easy watering have been marketed and are a great boon.

CARE

Potting or repotting a basket plant is the same as transplanting any indoor plant and is discussed in Chapter 9. If you would rather not do your own potting, florists will, for a fee, do it for you in your chosen container.

Once plants are in place you will want to know how to water them. If you cannot find the pulley device, the best way to water the plant is to use a long-beaked watering can. If you still cannot reach the plant to water it, use a one-step kitchen ladder. When you water, water slowly, that is, pour in some water, wait, and then pour in more to be sure you do not overwater so much that the excess water overflows the saucer and stains furniture or floors.

Once a month remove the container from its moorings and soak it in a sink of water to the rim of the pot. This eliminates acids and salt buildup and contributes greatly to the health of the plant. At the same time, wipe away soot and dust from the leaves with a damp cloth. Do not use leaf-shining solutions. They can clog leaf pores.

CHOICE TRAILING PLANTS

Abutilon hybridum (flowering maple)
Adiantum cuneatum (delta maidenhair)
A. hispidulum
A. tenurum wrightii
Aeschynanthus speciosus (lipstick vine)
Asparagus sprengeri (emerald fern)
Begonia 'Cleopatra'

Redwood baskets are popular containers for ferns in informal settings. This one has slatted wood construction and a nice design. (Photo by J. Kramer) ABOVE

Ferns hanging in wire baskets appropriate to a kitchen add charm to this country atmosphere and frame the African violet collection at the window. (Photo by Matthew Barr) BELOW

B. 'Elsie M. Frey'

B. *limminghiana*

B. 'Shippy's Garland'

B. 'Skeezar'

Campanula isophylla

Chlorophytum elatum (spider plant)

Chysis laevis

Cissus rhombifolia (grape ivy)

Columnea arguta

Davallia fejeenis (rabbit's-foot fern)

Dendrobium pierardii

Dipladenia amoena (Mexican love vine)

Episcia (many)

Gynura aurantiaca (velvet plant)

Hoya carnosa (wax plant)

Nephrolepis exaltata varieties (Boston fern)

Plectranthus coleoides (Swedish ivy)

Polypodium polycarpon (hare's-foot fern)

Saxifraga sarmentosa (strawberry geranium)

Sedum morganianum (burro's tail)

Tolmiea menziesii (piggy-back plant)

Zebrina pendula (wandering Jew)

Zygocactus truncatus (Christmas cactus)

Massive hanging plants are spectacular in areas such as this vaulted ceiling. To pull the scene together, a Philodendron bipinnatifidum *is used in rear at right, and at left (front) is a* Monstera deliciosa. *Note the silhouette effect of all plants. (Hedrich Blessing photo; Alden B. Dow & Assoc., Architects)*

7 🍃

Artificial Lighting for Display Plants

The problem with using interior plants to accent corners and other dim areas of rooms has always been lack of light. But artificial light has opened new avenues for decorative indoor plants. Fluorescent light has been available for many years for growing plants, but the design of the tube necessitated awkward metal reflectors and there were and are still no pleasing fixtures for interiors to hold fluorescent lamps. This is not true with incandescent lights; there is an array of lovely fixtures suitable for almost any interior. Sophisticated incandescent and mercury vapor lamps can help keep a plant in good health and maintain it for years, and properly

Reflector floodlights keep this attractive indoor garden, a part of the living room, in fine health. Dracaena marginata *is the lovely branching plant at right; at the left is a tall bamboo palm* (Chamaedorea erumpens). *Ferns and flowering plants decorate the floor and balance is achieved with the hanging baskets. (Photo by Hedrich Blessing; Garber, Tweddel & Wheeler, Architects)*

lighted plants can become things of beauty as they constantly change their silhouettes against walls.

Plants can accent any area in a room and still receive the necessary light they need when you use the new incandescent lamps and fixtures especially for plants. Fixtures can be placed on ceiling tracks or against walls, and because installation is not time-consuming, an electrician will not charge that much to put the system in working order. However, remember to tell the installer to put in a separate circuit for the plant lights because most plants need about 12 to 14 hours of artificial light.

FIXTURES

As mentioned previously, years ago, lighting large indoor plants was difficult because there were few attractive fixtures or simple methods of installing them. Usually the fittings for the fixtures had to be made at the time the house was under construction, and most fixtures were of institutional design and thus hardly pleasing in the home.

Today the lighting industry has responded with an array of handsome fixtures that can be used in any room with any decor. Usually the basic display-lighting fixture is a bullet- or cone-shaped unit mounted on a wall or ceiling. You can also use the new lighting tracks that allow you to set fixtures wherever you want them.

Track-system lighting consists of a strip of hardware mounted on ceiling or wall. Contemporary-styled fixtures can be attached to the track at any given point and angled in many directions. If you have a large indoor plant in a corner without light above it, a simple procedure is to use another fixture and attach it to the track (and you can do this yourself). Another advantage of track lighting is that it can be installed after the house is completed (with little ratification). These portable display-lighting fixtures (Power Trac by Halo Lighting Company and Lite-Span by Lightolier

A bathroom greenery under lights. Plants grow well here because
there is both natural and artificial light as well as abundant
humidity. The indoor garden is a conglomerate of houseplants:
philodendrons, rubber trees, ferns . . . a fine lovely setting.
(Hedrich Blessing photo; Charles W. Johnson, Architect)

A schefflera is shown to full dramatic effect in this room with the special spotlights to illuminate leaf edges. This is a unique and interesting way to use plants and lights. Notice also the use of the row of ferns to hide the light fixtures from view. ABOVE

Track lighting, such as shown here, solves many plant problems because fixtures are easily attached anywhere on the track and also can be moved to reflect light at almost any angle. (Photo courtesy Halo Lighting Co.) LEFT

Floodlights provide ample light for this corner greenery. Without artificial light here plants would not survive. The plants are rubber trees, Dracaena marginata, *philodendron, and dieffenbachias. (Photo courtesy General Electric Co.)*

Company) can be used in straight lines or in an infinite variety of patterns to cover almost any desired plant area. The hardware is sleek and blends well with almost any indoor setting; it is to be seen as well as used.

LAMPS

Use floodlamps to light your plants; spotlights strike only one area of the plant, but floods illuminate almost the entire plant, depending upon its size. Keep the incandescent or mercury vapor lamps at least 3 feet from the plant so there is no possibility of leaf burn from excessive heat. Use a 150- or 250-watt lamp (these lamps are generally available from most suppliers). An electrician should do the initial installation of the track; you can easily put in additional lamps if you so desire. The fixtures attach to the track with a unique adapter connector, which you twist to lock the fixture into position. This provides a polarized electrical connection. There are dozens of designs and sizes, and what you use depends upon your budget and taste.

PLANTS FOR ARTIFICIAL LIGHT GROWING

Here are some plants that do very well under 150-watt incandescent flood-lamps:

Agave americana marginata (century plant). Broad lance-shaped leaves; bold accent. Easy to grow; needs large container.

Araucaria excelsa (Norfolk pine). Can grow to 7 feet; looks like a Christmas tree.

Chamaedorea erumpens (bamboo palm). A large palm that looks like a fern. An absolute stellar room plant.

Dieffenbachia bowmannii. Chartreuse foliage.

D. hoffmannii. Showy white leaf pattern.

D. picta 'Rudolph Roehrs'. Arching leaves in shades of green.

D. splendens. Velvety green foliage with white dots.

Dizygotheca elegantissima (spider aralia). Dark green scalloped leaves edged in red in frond growth; tall, reedlike stems. To 60 inches.

Dracaena fragrans massangeana (corn plant). Cream-colored stripes on broad leaves. Grows somewhat like a palm from a central core and becomes a handsome tree in a few years.

D. godseffiana. Green leaves spattered with yellow; bushy growth, small size.

D. marginata. Well known and very expensive. Branching plant with compounds of sword-shaped leaves. Stellar.

D. sanderiana. Gray-green white margined foliage. Especially good for dish gardens.

Ferns. Large group, with many medium-sized stellar plants. Includes species of Adiantum, Asplenium, Davallia, and Nephrolepis.

Ficus benjamina (banyan tree). To 8 feet; small, lacy, delicate leaves.

F. elastica decora (rubber tree). Oval, glossy green leaves with ivory veins. To 60 inches.

F. retusa. Another good ficus.

Howea fosteriana (kentia palm). Graceful fronds with slender stalks. Slow growing; does well indoors.

Pandanus veitchii (screw pine). A spiral arrangement of long glossy green leaves. Handsome; amenable plant.

Philodendron bipinnatifidum. Large, deeply lobed leaves on arching stems. Always handsome. To 48 inches.

P. pertusum (Swiss cheese plant). Big and bold, with massive leaves.

P. wendlandii. Broad, dark green leaves in a compact rosette. To 40 inches in diameter.

Pittosporum tobira variegata. Tongue-shaped, rich green leaves edged in white. Compact growth to 40 inches.

Podocarpus macrophylla maki. Rich, green, tufted-type leaves in compact growth. To 30 inches.

Rhapis excelsa (lady palm). A handsome palm, with dark green, almost brittle, leaves on tall stems. Grows dense and massive with good care. To 30 inches.

Schefflera (Brassaia) actinophylla (umbrella tree). A tall branching plant with leaflets that form small canopies. Hardy and tolerant of indoor conditions. Can grow into small tree.

Yucca aloifolia (Spanish dagger). Pointed erect leaves make this a dramatic plant for room decor. Robust and strong and can live for a dozen years. Grows to 48 inches.

8 🍂

Containers and Plant Furniture

In recent years we have had not only new plants provided by suppliers but also an array of new containers. Once the clay pot and little else were all that was available for plants, but today any nursery has pots and tubs in all sizes in dozens of materials. Now, selecting the proper container is almost as important as choosing the right plant. Some containers are very ornamental with outside scrollwork or bas-relief designs. Be sure the design of the pot does not clash with the room furnishings.

Some plants, those with dark leaves such as *Philodendron hastatum* or *Ficus lyrata*, are more harmonious in a dark-colored container—a terracotta pot, for example, which is medium dark in value. In a white pot, the

These handsome rattan boxes are well suited for the bamboo trees (left) or for false aralia (right). (Photo courtesy McGuire Furniture Co.)

effect would be jarring to the eye. On the other hand, pale yellow-green sedums would be fine in white or straw-colored pots because color values match.

The standard clay pot is still with us, but in new designs and sizes. There are also fine glazed pots, ceramic containers, wooden tubs and pots, plastic and metal ones, jardinieres, and so forth for plants.

CLAY POTS

The clay pot is still one of the most functional housings for a plant because plants grow well in them and the natural clay color harmonizes with most indoor furnishings. These containers are available in a number of designs:

1. The simple and handsome Italian pot modifies the border to a tight-lipped detail. Some of these pots have rounded edges, and others are beveled or rimless, in sizes from 12 to 24 inches. These pots are decorative and blend well with contemporary settings.

2. Venetian pots are barrel-shaped, with a concentric band design pressed into the sides in a scored texture. They are somewhat formal in appearance, so use them with discretion.

3. Spanish pots are graceful, with outward sloping sides and flared lips in sizes from 8 to 20 inches. These pots have heavier walls than conventional clay ones and look good in period rooms.

4. Azalea or fern pots are squatty, limited in size to 14 inches, and generally fine for most rooms. They are a visual relief from the standard vase-shaped pot.

5. Cylindrical pots are new, and these terra-cotta containers are indeed handsome—a departure from the traditional tapered designs. They look well in almost any situation and come in four sizes, the maximum being 16 inches in diameter.

Handcrafted pottery can add yet another dimension to rooms.
The colors are earthy and natural; plants look striking in them;
and they blend well with most interiors.

Soy kegs are excellent containers where an informal look is wanted. Low bushy plants are suitable for them; be sure bottoms of kegs are secure in place when you purchase the containers. (Photo by Joyce R. Wilson)

Gold-leaf pots are indeed attractive but should be used with care. They have a sophisticated and elegant air, and if not chosen properly can clash with settings. (Photo by Joyce R. Wilson)

Here is an array of fine planters—some ornate,
others simple. Choose the one
that fits the plant and the room as
well. (Photo courtesy Architectural Pottery)

OTHER CONTAINERS

Although the unglazed pot is most popular, glazed containers have merit too. They offer the buyer a variety of colors, from black to brown to green. Because they can be overpowering, especially in large sizes, choose them carefully. White is always good for most interior color schemes, but some of the brighter colors may clash. Most glazed pots do not have drainage holes, so watering plants in them must be done moderately; overwatering can result in soggy soil that can kill plants. If you purchase decorative pots without drainage holes, take them to a glass store in your area and have holes drilled, or merely slip a potted plant into one of them.

Clear plastic pots have a simple elegance that makes them desirable in rooms. Three or four plants in plastic containers make a fine decoration for a kitchen sill or a dining room sideboard. However, plastic pots have a disadvantage, because in them large plants have a tendency to tip over.

Spun-steel or aluminum containers are another type of pot for plants. These are sleek and contemporary and must be used carefully in the home. They come with drainage holes and saucers, making them especially desirable. Try them for something special in a room.

Reed, wicker, or bamboo baskets are other unique containers (or more properly, coverups). Use the pot-in-a-pot method rather than planting directly in the basket. Place a saucer at the base of the basket (to catch excess water), and then insert the potted plant. Wicker, reed, and bamboo are very natural materials and blend well with almost any organic background; indeed, like the standard terra-cotta pots, these are containers that seem to harmonize well with any room setting. The baskets come in all shapes—square, rectangular, oval, and round, and thus offer limitless possibilities for one-of-a-kind plant decoration for interiors.

Japanese soy tubs and sawed-off wine casks are other unique containers. However, they do not fit every setting and must be chosen carefully or they will be out of place. If your rooms are rustic and informal, use them, but they are likely to be out of place in traditional or period rooms.

The blue glazed Japanese urns are stunning and can be special accents in an area. They are elegant and fit in beautifully with contemporary or period interiors. Brass pots and gold-leaf tubs are also fine for that special place.

BOXES AND TUBS

These are wooden containers, usually made from redwood or cypress. They are attractive for outdoors, but they are not (except in rare cases) good indoors. Eventually the wood rots and becomes unsightly because of water stain and acids. However, recently acrylic-coated redwood containers have made their appearance; these handsome pots are fine for some rooms. They are sleek and harmonize with more contemporary interiors and come in several sizes and shapes.

Concrete and concrete-type tubs are offered in many designs. Generally these do not come off well in most rooms, and they are extremely heavy, making them very difficult to move.

PLANT FURNITURE

Although floor plants are fine for many places in the home, invariably there will come a time when, because of space or as an accessory to an interior, you might want only a few medium-sized plants. Plant stands that take little space but still accommodate several plants are the answer; they are available as sleek metal and glass shelving or étagères, wrought-iron stands specifically designed for plants, or perhaps even a small ladder painted a suitable color to hold plants. The plant-stand garden is for a grouping of plants; pedestal tables and stands are for a single, somewhat large, plant, for example, a fern.

This is a simple elegant design; the container blends well with most room decors. Ferns such as the Pteris type shown here are well suited for the pots. (Photo courtesy Architectural Pottery)

A handsome bronze container in a rattan and rawhide stand. This special container deserves a handsome plant such as this dracaena and a special place in a room to show it off to its best effect. (Photo courtesy McGuire Furniture Co.)

You can also use glass or Plexiglas shelving to hold a few plants as a room accent. These are generally contemporary in design, and the green accent of plants is just right for contrast. Use three or four plants spaced accordingly, depending upon how many shelves there are rather than just one or two plants. Place the plants to either the front or the rear but not in the center, because there they invariably seem out of proportion to the total shelf unit. Wooden shelf units are also available, but these are bulky, and plants even on saucers will leave water stains on wood. Glass or Plexiglas shelves allow light to reach all plants, but wood might block light.

Wrought-iron stands that look like small spiral staircases are also fine for plants. These are now available at suppliers. Shelves are adjustable and generally accommodate one plant. And there is little chance of stain with wrought iron. Place these stands near windows or wherever you need an accent.

Wooden pedestals come in all shapes and sizes, antique or new, Greek or Chinese in character. They hold only one plant. These stands are part of the room furnishings and so should be chosen to match other furniture in a room. Some are lightweight in appearance, others—the antique types—are heavy and more dominant. For small rooms use the lightweight stand; for larger rooms the old stands make a nice accent.

Plants for stands and pedestals will be different in size and character than large-room plants. Generally, a medium- to small-sized plant is what you want, and it should be in proportion to the stand. For example, a large fern on a small pedestal is out of place. Keep the elements of design in mind: proportion, balance, and harmony.

Plant platforms—either small pedestals or homemade wooden stands—can be used to elevate floor plants to the desired height. Some are available commercially, but you will have to make most of them or have your local carpenter make them for you. Round plant platforms are better for most plants than square or rectangular ones, although the latter can be used if they fit the room decor.

These simple and elegant plant pedestals could blend with most room settings. Here they create a break between the two levels of the room. Pedestals with luxuriant trailing plants also make fine room accents. (Photo courtesy McGuire Furniture Co.)

9 🍂

Plant Care

Houseplants can be classified as those that require coolness and those that need warmth. However, even within these categories some plants will adjust to less than optimum conditions. But every plant needs light and will not grow or even live for more than a few weeks without it. Some plants prefer a sunny east or south window, others are best in a west exposure, and many foliage plants—schefflera and bromeliads, for example—make lovely greenery in north light. Select your plants accordingly. Wherever you place plants, turn them regularly; otherwise they become one-sided as they reach toward the source of light. African violet enthusiasts even advise a quarter turn every day!

Iron plant stands with several holders are convenient for displaying many plants in a confined area. (Photo by Morley Baer)

For most plants humidity (air moisture) of 30 to 40 percent is adequate, and almost all living rooms should provide this much for people and furniture as well as plants. Humidity can be increased as described later in this chapter for species requiring more. Fresh air is also essential to healthy plants even in very cold weather (but drafts are not!). Some plants need a great deal of care; others grow almost, but never entirely, untended.

SOILS

A good porous soil with adequate nutrients is essential for plant growth. I use 1 part garden loam to 1 part sand to 1 part leaf mold for most plants. For cacti, succulents, and some euphorbias I allow almost one-half instead of one-third sand. I put in peat moss for the acid-loving camellias and also for the anthuriums and tuberous begonias that need a moist condition. Peat moss is decomposed spongelike vegetable matter. It is rich in carbon, and absorbs and retains ten to twenty times its weight in water. It prevents soil from caking and helps to aerate it, so if you are forgetful about watering plants, peat moss can help keep soil moist. Orchids and bromeliads need osmunda (chopped roots of various ferns) or fir bark (steamed pieces of evergreen bark). All these materials are available in small sacks at nurseries.

Commercially packaged soil is good for many plants, particularly African violets and begonias, but do not use it for all plants. For example, cacti and succulents require a sandy soil, and ferns a loose porous soil. (Remember also that it is expensive if much is needed.) A better soil mixture can usually be bought by the bushel from a greenhouse. It is sterilized and has all the necessary ingredients for plant growth. You can use it as is or alter it to the needs of your own plants; that is, if it is not porous enough, you can add more sand, and if it feels thin and without body, put in more leaf mold or other humus.

Cornell University has developed growing mediums that contain no soil; they are called peatlite. I find this medium excellent for seedlings and, because it is lightweight, advantageous for big plants in tubs. But if you use it, be sure to give supplemental feeding of a water-soluble fertilizer every other watering through the growing season. Potting procedure with the peatlite mix is the same as with standard soils.

Soil from the garden usually contains weeds, insects, grubs, and bacteria that can cause disease in plants. Sterilizing the soil avoids these hazards. It is a messy, smelly procedure, but it can be done. Put dry soil through a fine sieve into a pan of water; do not pack it. Put the pan on the stove and turn up the heat until the water boils; then simmer for a few minutes. Turn out the soil into a clean baking dish and let it dry out. Or you can bake moistened soil in your oven in a roasting pan for 2 hours at 200°F. In either case, let the soil cool for 24 hours before use.

POTTING AND REPOTTING

Repotting is the transferring of a plant from one pot to another, usually to a larger one. Anyone decorating with houseplants should learn how to pot plants properly, because most small plants need new soil every year. For good growth give plants proper potting. Select a container neither too large nor too small in relation to the size of a specimen. This is necessary not only for esthetic reasons but also for the good of the plant. A small plant in a large pot is apt to suffer because unused soil can become soggy and harm roots.

To pot a plant, use a clean container. New clay pots should be soaked overnight in water before use or they will draw undue moisture from the soil of new plantings. Scrub old pots with steel wool soap pads and hot water and rinse thoroughly to remove any accumulation of algae or salts.

Put an arching piece or two of broken pot (shards) over the drainage hole to keep in soil. Spread porous stones over the shards, along with a few pieces of charcoal (charcoal keeps the soil sweet). Then place the plant in the center of the pot, holding it in position with one hand, and fill in and around it with a fresh soil mixture with the other hand. Firm soil around the stem with your thumbs. To settle the soil and eliminate air spaces, strike the base of the pot on a table a few times. A properly potted plant can be lifted by the stem without being loosened.

Leave about an inch of space at the top between pot rim and soil to receive water. Water newly potted plants thoroughly; then for a few days keep them in a light rather than sunny place. They can be moved once they are accustomed to brightness. Label all plants; it is nice to know what you are growing. When roots push through the drainage hole in a pot or appear on the surface it is time to give the plant more root room and to replenish the soil. An exact schedule for repotting is not possible; plants in large pots (over 24 inches) can go 2 years without fresh soil, but smaller potted plants need soil every year. If you fertilize regularly, thus replacing soil nutrients, many plants can stay in the same pot longer than if they are not fed, but they must be leached periodically. Soak them to the rim in a sink of water for 1 hour to leach out acids and salts.

To check the possible need for a larger pot, hold your hand over the soil (it should be slightly moist), keeping the main stem between your fingers. Invert the pot and knock the rim sharply against the edge of a shelf or table. Rap the base also; the whole rootball will then drop easily into your hand. If it is covered with a network of roots, the plant needs a larger pot. When you shift a plant to a smaller or larger pot, crumble away as much old soil from the roots as possible without harming the roots.

Specimens in very large containers, more than 14 inches across, or in permanent planters such as room dividers, are best left undisturbed as long as possible. To recondition them, dig out 3 to 4 inches of surface soil and replace it with a fertile fresh mixture. (This process is called "top dressing.")

WATERING AND FEEDING

How and when you water depends upon the type of pot used, where you live, and the kind of plant. Generally, no plant should be allowed to go completely dry (even during semidormancy); and no plant should be kept in soggy soil because it can create a sour condition that can cause roots to rot. If soil is too dry, plant roots become dehydrated and growth stops. Continuously wet soil becomes sour and roots rot.

Some plants prefer an evenly moist soil; others, such as begonias and clivias, grow best in soil that is allowed to approach dryness between waterings. Cacti and some other succulents may be permitted to become almost completely dry.

When you water, allow excess water to pour from the drainage hole; the complete root system must get moisture. It is harmful if only the top soils gets wet and the lower part stays dry because then the soil usually turns sour and growth is retarded.

Water of room temperature is best. If possible, water in the morning so the soil can dry out before evening. Lingering moisture and cool nights are an invitation to fungus diseases.

Most plants benefit from feeding; however, bromeliads and flowering plants such as many orchids are slow growing and feeding can harm them. Commercial man-made fertilizers contain some nitrogen, an element that stimulates foliage growth, but too much can retard development of flower buds. Fertilizers also contain phosphorus, which promotes root and stem development and stimulates bloom, and potash, which promotes health, stabilizes growth, and intensifies color. The ratio of elements is marked on the package or bottle in this order: nitrogen, phosphorus, potash. There are many formulas; I prefer 10-10-5 for most houseplants. You can also use organic fertilizers, and I highly prescribe these: bone meal, cottonseed meal and fish emulsion.

New plants and ailing plants do not require feeding. New ones in fresh soil have adequate nutrients and do not need more; ailing plants are not capable of absorbing nutrients. After they flower, allow plants to rest for a few weeks. Water only occasionally, and do not feed. A safe rule is to fertilize only the plants that are in active growth.

Foliar feeding, that is, applying fertilizer to the leaves in a water solution, is often recommended. However, hairy-leaved plants like some begonias and African violets object to lingering moisture on leaves, especially if the solution is not of room temperature. My best results have been with commercial soluble fertilizer applied to the soil.

HEAT AND HUMIDITY

Cool-preference plants such as campanulas and hoyas need 54° to 58° F at night, 10 to 15 degrees more during the day. Warm growers like anthuriums and most begonias require 64° to 68° F at night, 72° to 80° F during the day. With few exceptions, most plants fall into one of these groups. In other words, average home temperatures suit most plants.

In winter it is necessary to protect plants from extreme cold. On very cold nights, put cardboard or newspapers between plants and windows to mitigate the chill of the glass.

Although automatic humidifiers are now part of many heating systems, older apartment houses and buildings do not have this advantage. Humidity—the amount of moisture in the air—should be at a healthful level for both people and plants. A humidity gauge (a hygrometer) registers the amount of relative humidity. The average humidity for most homes is 30 to 40 percent, which is good for most plants. However, some plants like clivias and philodendrons will grow in low humidity, say 30 percent; others, such as rechsteinerias and gloxinias, require 70 to 80 percent humidity.

The difficulty with humidity is keeping it in proper relation to artificial and summer heat. Balance is the key factor to good plant growth. The hotter it is, the faster air dries out. Because plants take up water through roots and release it through leaves, they give off moisture faster when the surrounding air is dry than when it is damp. If they lose water quicker than they can replace it, foliage becomes thin and depleted. When summer heat is at its peak, between 11 A.M. and 1 P.M., spray plants lightly with water. For years a 15¢ window-cleaning bottle for misting plants was essential equipment for me. Now new sprayers on the market give better misting than my old-fashioned gadget. Made under various trade names, these hand-operated fog-makers have plastic noncorrosive washable containers and come in 16- or 32-ounce sizes. They dispense a fine mist that is beneficial for almost all plants, cleansing the foliage and, for a brief time anyway, increasing the humidity.

In winter, when artificial heat is high, between 6 P.M. and 8 P.M., provide more air moisture. Turn on your room humidifier, or mist pots and soil surface but not foliage; at night wet foliage is an invitation to disease.

In addition to misting, plants can also be set on wet gravel in, say, a 3-inch-deep large metal or Fiberglas tray. This furnishes some additional humidity. Plants can also be placed on pebble-filled saucers; keep stones constantly moist.

Strong growth and firm leaves (assuming temperature and light are in proper proportion) are signs of good humidity. Spindly growth and limp leaves usually indicate too little moisture in the air. Keep plants away from hot radiators and blasts of hot air and also out of drafts.

FRESH AIR AND AIR CONDITIONING

Plants grown in rooms where there is a good circulation of air do better than plants in a closed atmosphere. Let outside air into rooms where plants are growing whenever possible. In winter, when artificial heat can be extreme, the air is drier than outside; ventilation will help maintain desirable humidity. If it is impossible to open windows where the plants are growing, see to it that there is adequate ventilation in an adjoining room. But always avoid admitting cold air drafts that blow directly on the plants.

Air conditioning is a boon to people who suffer in hot summer climates. Most plants, too, resent torrid weather. Many houseplants like bougainvillaeas and rhizomatous begonias suffer when temperatures soar. I have seen bromeliads and palms in excellent health in public buildings with central air conditioning. I thought that the low humidity which prevails with artificial cooling might harm plants, but they did not show signs of poor growth from the lack of moisture in the air. Uniform temperatures seem to be far more beneficial than the hot and cold extremes of summer. However, cold air from wall or window air conditioners directed at plants can harm them. Drafts have a desiccating effect because they cause excessive loss of moisture; leaves wilt or turn yellow and fall.

SEASONAL CARE

A controlling factor of plant growth, indoors and out, is weather. The cycle of the year—spring, summer, autumn, winter—influences plant growth. Remember that the majority of houseplants do most of their growing in spring and summer, so this is when watering should be heavy. Also repot old plants in February and March so they have a chance to take advantage of moderate weather. Be sure that plants are ready for the warming trend. New soil with adequate nutrients starts them off right, and adequate humidity and regular watering keeps them healthy.

Most plants grow rapidly in summer, even indoors. Some, such as columneas and fuchsias, need plenty of moisture at the roots, at least once and, if necessary, twice a day. Feed plants that are in active growth. Protect them from noonday sun, which may be too strong for most of them.

Usually a window screen is enough, but in the South a thin curtain may be required. Watch out for pests, and provide good ventilation and humidity. Avoid a stuffy atmosphere. On very hot days mist plants several times to reduce heat.

Fall brings changing weather—some hot days, some cool ones—a crucial time for houseplants. Water with care, each plant according to its need. With many plants, such as fuchsias, hedychiums, and oleanders, growth has matured by winter and they are in a semidormant condition. Stop feeding; never try to force resting plants to sprout fresh leaves. Let the soil go somewhat dry but not so dry that it gets caked.

WHEN PLANTS REST

A plant is a living organism, and like people who sleep to regain energy, plants rest at some time of year, growing much more slowly or not at all, and flowering kinds stop setting buds. This dormancy is vital. Many of the plants we grow indoors—orchids, bromeliads, and hypocyrtas—come from climates with sharply defined seasons of rain and drought. Though far removed from their habitat, their cycles of growth remain the same, and we must respect them if we are to be successful.

In general most plants need less moisture or none at all for a short period at some time of year. Of course there are exceptions. Many plants rest a little after flowering unless they are kinds that make heavy foliage growth then, such as clerodendrums. Summer-flowering plants have a fairly dormant period in winter. But some plants, given good culture, bloom continuously, for example, the African violet.

Usually plants plainly indicate their need for rest. You will see signs of declining vigor. Unless a plant is suffering from some pest or disease, encourage it to slow down. Gradually reduce watering and, of course, stop fertilizing.

PLANT PROBLEMS

If you buy healthy plants and give them reasonable care, there will be few insects. Observation is the other key to success in avoiding pests on plants. Sometimes, however, the decline of a plant is improper culture rather than alien invaders. So first look to your cultural methods before running to buy insecticides. Plants give clues if they are not happy: brown or yellow leaves, pale weak growth or slow growth, or falling leaves. Any of these conditions can be caused by heat or humidity too low or too high, temperature extremes, not enough or too much light, or sour old soil.

To keep your plants healthy groom them well; pick off dead leaves and faded flowers. Wipe or mist foliage with warm water once a week to remove insect eggs and spider mites, to generally discourage other pests, and to keep leaf pores open. (Plants breathe through their leaves so do not use leaf-shining preparations.) Once a month (if at all possible) soak plants to the pot rim in a sink to eliminate any toxic salts that build up from feeding. This is impossible with large plants because they are difficult to move. But they can be moved outdoors; leach the soil with a hose. Even with good culture some plants may be invaded by insects, but this is no reason to panic; there are easy ways of eliminating unwanted guests. First identify the culprits. Basically there will be only a few kinds of insects that might attack plants: (1) aphids—soft-bodied green, black, or red ⅛-inch oval insects; (2) mealybugs—easily recognized as cottony white clusters in stems and axils; and (3) scale—little brown, white, or gray oval pests.

Your best prevention, if you do not like poisons in the home, is a solution of laundry soap and water. Douse insects three times a week until they give up. You can also use a Q-Tip dipped in alcohol for mealybugs, and many times scale can be picked off plants with a toothpick.

If insect problems still persist after home remedies (or you do not have time for them), use nicotine sulfate (Black Leaf 40) applied as directed on the package. This old-time preventative is good for a number of insects. It is poison, however, so handle with caution, and keep it out of the reach of children and pets.

Systemics—insecticides applied to the soil—will eliminate many but not all kinds of insects. One application will protect plants (except palms and ferns) from the majority of sucking insects for 6 to 8 weeks. Systemics come in granular form; sprinkle the powder over soil and then water the plant thoroughly. Keep your plants healthy; insects generally attack weak plants rather than strong-growing well ones.

INDEX